OUR GOD
and HIS
CHILDREN

CLARENCE SEXTON

CROWN
CHRISTIAN
PUBLICATIONS
Royal Reading

FAITHFORTHEFAMILY.COM

Our God and His Children

FIRST EDITION
COPYRIGHT
MAY 2005

CROWN
CHRISTIAN
PUBLICATIONS
Royal Reading

FAITHFORTHEFAMILY.COM

PILLAR
AND GROUND
OF THE TRUTH
CHURCH PLANTING AND
SUNDAY SCHOOL SERIES

OUR GOD AND HIS CHILDREN

Copyright © 2005
Crown Christian Publications
Powell, Tennessee 37849
CrownChristianPublications.com
FaithfortheFamily.com
ISBN: 1-58981-266-2

Layout by Stephen Troell & Reynaldo Pepin

Printed in the United States of America

Dedication

This book is affectionately dedicated to my dear friend Tim Cruse. Tim is a faithful family man.

He is the pastor of a wonderful church and has a heart for God. His friendship continues to be a source of tremendous encouragement to me.

Clarence Sexton

Acts 5:42

Contents

CHAPTER ONE — THE BLESSED MAN.................................9

CHAPTER TWO — WHY DO THE HEATHEN RAGE............................23

CHAPTER THREE — THE LORD SUSTAINED ME....................................35

CHAPTER FOUR — WHEN THE LORD ENLARGES US........................47

CHAPTER FIVE — LEAD ME, O LORD.................................57

CHAPTER SIX — FOR THY MERCIES' SAKE....................................71

CHAPTER SEVEN — MY DEFENCE IS OF GOD.....................................85

CHAPTER EIGHT — WHAT IS MAN?....................................101

CHAPTER NINE — ALL THE NATIONS THAT FORGET GOD...............119

CHAPTER TEN — IN TIMES OF TROUBLE......................................131

CHAPTER ELEVEN — IF THE FOUNDATIONS BE DESTROYED.............145

CHAPTER TWELVE — HELP, LORD...157

CHAPTER THIRTEEN — HAS GOD FORGOTTEN YOU?...............................165

PSALM 1

Blessed is the man that walketh not in the counsel of the ungodly, nor standeth in the way of sinners, nor sitteth in the seat of the scornful.

But his delight is in the law of the LORD; and in his law doth he meditate day and night.

And he shall be like a tree planted by the rivers of water, that bringeth forth his fruit in his season; his leaf also shall not wither; and whatsoever he doeth shall prosper.

The ungodly are not so: but are like the chaff which the wind driveth away.

Therefore the ungodly shall not stand in the judgment, nor sinners in the congregation of the righteous.

For the LORD knoweth the way of the righteous: but the way of the ungodly shall perish.

CHAPTER ONE

nter into the heart of God. The Bible is a Book about God. It is His written revelation of Himself to us. No book brings us nearer to God than the Psalms. So enter in with much prayer. Seek Him. Meet Him in His Word.

The book of Psalms is a most blessed book. The key verse for the book of Psalms is found in Psalm 29:2. God says, *"Give unto the LORD the glory due unto his name; worship the LORD in the beauty of holiness."*

The Psalms are quoted more often in the New Te stament than any other book in the Old Testament. Of the one hundred and fifty Psalms, one-third are anonymous. Seventy-three of the Psalms are attributed to David, twelve to Asaph, eleven to the sons of Korah, two to Solomon, and one to Moses. The Psalm of Moses is Psalm 90. It is the oldest of the Psalms.

There are five divisions in the book of Psalms. The last psalm in each division closes with blessing and glory to God. The first division is Psalm 1-41. The second is Psalm 42-72. The third is Psalm 73-89. The fourth is Psalm 90-106. The fifth is Psalm 107-150.

Consider the Psalms as one book, but take the time to prayerfully read the concluding psalm, considering each division, comparing Scripture with Scripture. As we look at the very first Psalm, it is as though God gives us a preface for the entire book of Psalms. In the first Psalm, we are given a foundation on which to place all the other psalms.

When you hold the Bible in your hand, you hold the most wonderful Book known to man. It is one Book with one Author, the Holy Spirit. Human instruments were used to pen the words, but it is the Book that God wrote. Men were moved along by the Spirit of God to pen the words as God revealed His Word to them. The Scriptures were given by inspiration of God.

The Bible is divided into the Old Testament and the New Testament. When we have the Old Testament open before us, we know there are five books in the beginning of the Old Testament that deal with the Law. We call these five books the Pentateuch. Moses was the human penman for the Pentateuch. These five books are followed by twelve historical books. After the historical books, in the heart of the Old Testament, we have five books written in poetical form: Job, Psalms, Proverbs, Ecclesiastes, and the Song of Solomon. On the other side of those five books are the five books of the major prophets and twelve books of the minor prophets.

As we look into the heart of the Old Testament at the five poetic books, we find that these books do not deal with the great national issues of Israel or some other country, but with the heart issues of mankind.

Let us consider the very first Psalm. Psalm 1:1-6 says,

> *Blessed is the man that walketh not in the counsel*
> *of the ungodly, nor standeth in the way of sinners,*

nor sitteth in the seat of the scornful. But his delight is in the law of the LORD; and in his law doth he meditate day and night. And he shall be like a tree planted by the rivers of water, that bringeth forth his fruit in his season; his leaf also shall not wither; and whatsoever he doeth shall prosper. The ungodly are not so: but are like the chaff which the wind driveth away. Therefore the ungodly shall not stand in the judgment, nor sinners in the congregation of the righteous. For the LORD knoweth the way of the righteous: but the way of the ungodly shall perish.

Note the first expression, *"Blessed is the man."* In this first Psalm, God gives us in the first three verses a portrait of the blessed man. Who is a blessed man? The blessed man is the man that God honors and blesses.

Do you desire to be a blessed man? I want to live my life with His blessing and honor. Satan uses all kinds of things to distract us, but I pray that God will help me not to be sidetracked by anything that will keep me from being the blessed man that God desires for me to be. It is a joy and wonder, but a truth, that God desires to bless me. He desires that I be a blessed man.

As we begin reading through our Bible and we come to the story of the life of Abraham, God says, *"I will bless thee."* Here is the covenant that God made with Abraham. We call this covenant the Abrahamic covenant. The Lord says to Abraham, *"I will bless thee."* It is right for each of us to desire to be one of those people whom God will bless. I want my life to be blessed because I know that if my life is blessed, my wife will be blessed because of my life. I want my life to be blessed because I know if my life is blessed, my children will be blessed. I want my life to be blessed because if my life is blessed, not only will my wife and children be blessed, but the work that I do for God will be blessed. I want to be a blessed man.

11

THE PROHIBITIONS

If we want to be blessed, there are certain prohibitions that are given to us. The Bible says in Psalm 1:1, *"Blessed is the man that walketh not in the counsel of the ungodly, nor standeth in the way of sinners, nor sitteth in the seat of the scornful."*

God says there are certain things that this blessed man is prohibited from doing if he is going to be blessed. Of course, there are some people who think that anything that is negative need not be even mentioned. However, there are definitely prohibitions in the Word of God that we must heed if we desire God's blessing.

In the twentieth chapter of the book of Exodus we find one of the most important passages in the Bible. The Bible says in Exodus 20:1-3, *"And God spake all these words, saying, I am the LORD thy God, which have brought thee out of the land of Egypt, out of the house of bondage. Thou shalt have no other gods before me."*

All of this is really the first of the Ten Commandments, but we usually quote only the first commandment from the third verse which says, *"Thou shalt have no other gods before me."*

In verse four we find the second commandment which says, *"Thou shalt not make unto thee any graven image."*

The commandments continue in verse seven, *"Thou shalt not take the name of the LORD thy God in vain."*

Verse eight says, *"Remember the sabbath day, to keep it holy."*

Verse twelve says, *"Honour thy father and thy mother."*

Verses thirteen through seventeen declare, *"Thou shalt not kill. Thou shalt not commit adultery. Thou shalt not steal. Thou shalt not bear false witness against thy neighbour. Thou shalt not covet."*

We need to understand that this is the Word of God. God has given certain prohibitions to man. There are things we cannot do if we want to be blessed of God.

There are things I cannot read if I want to be blessed of God. There are things my eyes cannot look upon if I desire to be blessed of God. There are places I cannot go if I want to be blessed of God. There are certain things I should never say if I want to be a blessed man. There are certain things I cannot take into my body if I want to be a blessed man. God has prohibited me from doing certain things if I want to be a blessed man.

In Psalm one the Bible says, *"Blessed is the man that walketh not in the counsel of the ungodly."* The blessed man does not seek counsel from the ungodly. This is a prohibition.

The Bible continues, *"...nor standeth in the way of sinners."* The way sinners are going is not the way the blessed man is going. He does not stand with those people. The Bible continues, *"...nor sitteth in the seat of the scornful."* Notice that first he is walking, then he stops to stand, and then he

THE TEN COMMANDMENTS

•

"Thou shalt have no other gods before me."

"Thou shalt not make unto thee any graven image."

"Thou shalt not take the name of the LORD thy God in vain."

"Remember the sabbath day, to keep it holy."

"Honour thy father and thy mother."

"Thou shalt not kill."

"Thou shalt not commit adultery."

"Thou shalt not steal."

"Thou shalt not bear false witness against thy neighbour."

"Thou shalt not covet."

sits down. I used to say this was a progression, but it is really a digression. He is first simply walking. Then he gets a little interested

in what is going on with sinners, and he stops and stands until finally he sits down. At that point you cannot tell any difference between him and all the sinners. God says He prohibits this. The blessed man does not walk in the counsel of the ungodly. The blessed man does not stand in the way of sinners. The blessed man does not sit in the seat of the scornful.

Let us apply this to where we live and work. If there are people in your place of business who have already identified themselves as people who give no regard to God, then if you desire to be a blessed man, you should obey this prohibition from God's Word. You should not walk, stand, or sit with them and be identified with their ungodliness. Have compassion on them, witness to them, seek to bring them to Christ, but do not lose your Christian testimony with them.

If you begin walking with them, you will stand with them, and before long you will be sitting with them, talking just like they talk, and behaving just as they behave.

The blessed man has certain prohibitions in his life. If we participate with sinners in their sinful behavior, we are never going to win them to Jesus Christ.

THE PECULIARITIES

The blessed man has some things that are peculiar to him. I call these things "peculiarities" because they are differences. The blessed man is not like everyone else in the world. He is a transformed man. He is changed from the inside out. He is not constantly attempting to conform to the world. The Bible says in Psalm 1:2-3, *"But his delight is in the law of the LORD; and in his law doth he meditate day and night. And he shall be like a tree planted by the rivers of water, that bringeth forth his fruit in his season; his leaf also shall not wither; and whatsoever he doeth shall prosper."*

14

This blessed man is not like the ungodly man. There are some things that are definitely different about his life. Notice what the Bible says about these peculiarities. The first thing the Bible says is that the blessed man delights in the Law of the Lord.

The ungodly do not delight in God's Word, but the blessed man delights in the Law of God. We should be sweet, kind, compassionate, and Christ-like, but we should take our stand for the Lord. We need to speak up about what we know from the Word of God. We are to speak kindly and compassionately, but boldly for Jesus Christ. People should know we are Christians because we delight in the truth of God's Word.

In every sphere of your life, people need to know that you are a Christian. In every place that you eat, people should know you are a Christian. Everyone who rides to work with you should know you are a Christian. Everyone who goes to school with you should know you are a Christian. The blessed man is identified as a believer because he delights in the Law of the Lord. He loves God's Word. He is guided by the Bible. He lives his life by the standards of God's Word.

Did you realize that we can be busy for God and not be blessed of God?

The Bible says in Psalm 37:1-4,

> *Fret not thyself because of evildoers, neither be thou envious against the workers of iniquity. For they shall soon be cut down like the grass, and wither as the green herb. Trust in the LORD, and do good; so shalt thou dwell in the land, and verily thou shalt be fed. Delight thyself also in the LORD; and he shall give thee the desires of thine heart.*

As we delight in the Lord, He places in our hearts the desires we need to have for His name's sake. We begin to desire from God what He has already desired for us. This is the beauty of the Christian life.

The apostle Paul wrote to the church in Philippi, *"For it is God which worketh in you both to will and to do of his good pleasure"* (Philippians 2:13). To *"will"* means to "desire." We could say, "It is God which worketh in you both to *desire* and to do of His good pleasure." The wonder of what I am doing is not that I am serving God; the wonder is that I *desire* to serve God. The Bible says if we delight in the Lord, the Lord will give us the desires of our heart. He will work in us to desire what is best from Him. The blessed man desires what is right because he delights in the Law of the Lord. Think of the power of this truth. What a transforming truth it is to desire from God what He desires for us.

In Psalm one the Bible says that the blessed man not only delights in the Law of the Lord, but also meditates in God's Word. *"In his law doth he meditate day and night."*

The Bible says in Joshua 1:8, *"This book of the law shall not depart out of thy mouth; but thou shalt meditate therein day and night, that thou mayest observe to do according to all that is written therein: for then thou shalt make thy way prosperous, and then thou shalt have good success."*

The blessed man meditates on the Word of God. He muses over the Word of God. He puts the Word of God in his heart, and he can recall it.

Did you realize that we can be busy for God and not be blessed of God? Did you know that you can be in every church service and not be a blessed man? Did you know that you could be in church Sunday morning, Sunday night, and Wednesday night and not be a blessed man? The blessed man delights in the Lord. The blessed man meditates on the Word of God. According to this psalm, the blessed man is *"like a tree that is planted."* Occasionally we see a

tree growing that no one planted. It just happened to spring up. Seed somehow was deposited, and it started growing. But the blessed man is not that way. God says he is like a planted tree. His life has purpose and design. God is in control.

The blessed man is not only planted, he is *"planted by the rivers of water."* Who is this water? The Lord Jesus is the water of life. He is the river.

The blessed man also *"bringeth forth his fruit in his season."* He is a fruitful man. It is possible to be active but not fruitful. It is possible to be involved but not fruitful. Not every tree in an orchard bears fruit. The blessed man is fruitful.

In John 15:1-2 the Lord Jesus said, *"I am the true vine, and my Father is the husbandman. Every branch in me that beareth not fruit he taketh away: and every branch that beareth fruit, he purgeth it..."* That purging is a necessary process that we do not enjoy, but that we must go through. Did you know that both people and churches are purged? Whatever God chooses to make fruitful must be purged.

This purging business is painful sometimes, but God wants us to bear fruit. The blessed man bears fruit. The Bible says, *"...he purgeth it, that it may bring forth more fruit."* Would you like to bear fruit or more fruit? If so, then there must be purging. The Bible continues in verses three through five,

> *Now ye are clean through the word which I have spoken unto you. Abide in me, and I in you. As the branch cannot bear fruit of itself, except it abide in the vine; no more can ye, except ye abide in me. I am the vine, ye are the branches: he that abideth in me, and I in him, the same bringeth forth much fruit: for without me ye can do nothing.*

According to the Bible, we can have fruit, more fruit, or much fruit, but the blessed man bears fruit. As we are working and planning, God says, "If you would just be a blessed man, I would make you fruitful."

Psalm one continues in verse three, *"...his leaf also shall not wither; and whatsoever he doeth shall prosper."* I would like to have this promise fulfilled in my life, that whatsoever I do will prosper. If you study the word *"prosper"* in the context of God's Word, I do not believe it can be confined to mean only material advantage. This is not a way to riches; it is the way to God's blessing on your life.

> *This is not a way to riches; it is the way to God's blessing on your life.*

The blessed man has certain prohibitions. There are things he cannot do. God says, "Don't do that if you desire to be a blessed man." God says there are certain things that are peculiar to the blessed man. He gives a list. When He gets near to the end of that list He says, "Whatever he does will prosper. You are going to see that My hand is on him."

People frequently call me and want me to recommend a man to pastor their church. They develop these long, detailed questionaires for men to fill out about being the pastor. They want to know what he believes about every doctrine in the Bible. They want to know where he has been and how long he has been there, where he has studied, who he knows, and who will recommend him. I tell these people when they call me, "You find a man who has God's hand on his life and call him to be your pastor. God will bless your church from the blessing that is on that man." God says of the blessed man, *"Whatsoever he doeth shall prosper."*

THE PROMISE

In the fourth verse of Psalm one the Bible says, *"The ungodly are not so: but are like the chaff which the wind driveth away."* The

chaff is the wasted part of the grain. In the winnowing process, the chaff is taken away by the wind.

As we think about the coming of the Lord, this wicked world would like to get rid of Christians. The *"chaff"* does not understand that if it were not for the Christian "wheat," the judgment of God would already be unleashed upon this unbelieving world. When this wheat is taken out and only the chaff is left, then the unleashing of the judgment of God is going to come on this unbelieving world. The Bible says that the ungodly are *"like the chaff which the wind driveth away."*

We read in Psalm 1:5-6, *"Therefore the ungodly shall not stand in the judgment, nor sinners in the congregation of the righteous. For the LORD knoweth the way of the righteous, but the way of the ungodly shall perish."*

There is no doubt that the only light the ungodly have is the little light they have here. They are going to hell. The only brightness, the only day, the only joy the ungodly have is what they can glean from this world. The Bible says they are going to perish.

Notice carefully the promise God makes to the blessed man. The Bible says, *"The LORD knoweth the way of the righteous."* This is His promise. God knows where we are. God knows our path. God knows exactly where we are on that path at any given moment. The promise is that God knows the way of the righteous.

In Job chapter twenty-three, we see Job under a terrible burden. It is as though he cannot find God. He needs God, but he cannot seem to get hold of Him. The Bible says in verses one through nine,

> *Then Job answered and said, Even today is my complaint bitter: my stroke is heavier than my groaning. Oh that I knew where I might find him! that I might come even to his seat! I would order my cause before him, and fill my mouth with arguments.*

19

I would know the words which he would answer me, and understand what he would say unto me. Will he plead against me with his great power? No; but he would put strength in me. There the righteous might dispute with him; so should I be delivered for ever from my judge. Behold, I go forward, but he is not there; and backward, but I cannot perceive him: on the left hand, where he doth work, but I cannot behold him: he hideth himself on the right hand, that I cannot see him.

Job says, "I am trying to find God. I need Him. Where is He?" Then he says in verse ten, *"But he knoweth the way that I take: when he hath tried me, I shall come forth as gold."*

God says, "I promise the blessed man this." There may be times in his life when he says, "Where is God in all this?" But God says, "At that moment you may not be able to find me, but I know your way. I can always find you. I know exactly where you are." The Lord knows the way of the righteous.

From the man-ward side, sometimes I have thought, "How in this world can I go on?" But from the God-ward side, for the blessed man, God is saying, "Don't fret or worry. I know where you are. Everything is still under control. I am going to see you through. I know your way." This is the promise of God to the blessed man. Oh! How we thank God for this precious promise!

Psalm 2:1-6

Why do the heathen rage, and the people imagine a vain thing?

The kings of the earth set themselves, and the rulers take counsel together, against the LORD and against his anointed, saying,

Let us break their bands asunder, and cast away their cords from us.

He that sitteth in the heavens shall laugh: the Lord shall have them in derision.

Then shall he speak unto them in his wrath, and vex them in his sore displeasure.

Yet have I set my king upon my holy hill of Zion.

CHAPTER TWO

WHY DO THE HEATHEN RAGE?

 salm two is a stirring psalm that goes hand in hand with the first Psalm and continues to lay the foundation for the entire book of Psalms. This is a Messianic psalm. This psalm exalts our Savior and gives prophetic references to our Lord Jesus Christ. Recognizing that this is a Messianic psalm enables us to understand its meaning. The Bible says in Psalm two,

> *Why do the heathen rage, and the people imagine a vain thing? The kings of the earth set themselves, and the rulers take counsel together, against the LORD, and against his anointed, saying, Let us break their bands asunder, and cast away their cords from us. He that sitteth in the heavens shall laugh: the Lord shall have them in derision. Then shall he speak unto them in his wrath, and vex them in his sore displeasure. Yet have I set my king upon my holy hill of Zion. I will declare the decree: the LORD hath said unto me, Thou art my*

Son; this day have I begotten thee. Ask of me, and I shall give thee the heathen for thine inheritance, and the uttermost parts of the earth for thy possession. Thou shalt break them with a rod of iron; thou shalt dash them in pieces like a potter's vessel. Be wise now therefore, O ye kings: be instructed, ye judges of the earth. Serve the LORD with fear, and rejoice with trembling. Kiss the Son, lest he be angry, and ye perish from the way, when his wrath is kindled but a little. Blessed are all they that put their trust in him.

Note the question given in the opening verse of this psalm, *"Why do the heathen rage?"* We know that the heathen rage, and we know that the people imagine vain things. However, the Lord raises this question for us in Scripture, arousing our interest and demanding an answer. Of course, we find the answer in the Word of God.

As long as you and I live in this world, people are going to say things that are not true. If we do not know the truth, many times those things are going to upset us; but if we know the truth, so much of what is said by an unbelieving world should not trouble us at all. This matter is settled in this second Psalm.

THE LOST ARE SPEAKING

In this psalm, the Bible says that the lost lift their voices with rage. The heathen are lost; they do not know the true and living God. They imagine a vain thing. We read in verse two, *"The kings of the earth set themselves, and the rulers take counsel together, against the LORD, and against his anointed."*

Remember that they are raging, not simply talking. They have come together to take counsel. They have united their forces *"against the LORD, and against his anointed."* The Bible records their words

24

in verse three, *"Let us break their bands asunder, and cast away their cords from us."*

The voice of the lost says, "We will not be bound by anything God says or anything God wants us to do. We want to break loose from every type of restraint that God can place upon us. We want to be free to speak and do as we please. We do not want God telling us what to do." This is the voice of the sin nature found in each of us.

The Bible says in the book of Jude verses ten through thirteen,

> But these speak evil of those things which they know not: but what they know naturally, as brute beasts, in those things they corrupt themselves. Woe unto them! for they have gone in the way of Cain, and ran greedily after the error of Balaam for reward, and perished in the gainsaying of Core. These are spots in your feasts of charity, when they feast with you, feeding themselves without fear: clouds they are without water, carried about of winds; trees whose fruit withereth, without fruit, twice dead, plucked up by the roots; raging waves of the sea, foaming out their own shame....

They are as *"raging waves of the sea."* When those who are against God speak, we should not be troubled by their words. When they make their raging speeches, we should not be upset and fret over what they have said. As they speak, all they are doing, according to the Bible, is *"foaming out their own shame."* They are revealing more about themselves than God.

In Jude 13, the Bible calls them *"wandering stars."* They are bright for a moment, but the Bible says they are *"wandering stars, to whom is reserved the blackness of darkness for ever."*

When these lost leaders gather together in Psalm two, they lift their voices against God and declare that they will not be bound.

God says they rage, and today we hear them raging. They are anti-God and anti-Bible. They stand against the truth of God's Word. What they say only demonstrates their shame. It demonstrates what is in their hearts.

For now we will have to listen to speeches that sound like the sea foaming out raging statements against God and against decency. All of this is just a foretaste of where the world is ultimately headed.

The Bible says they *"imagine a vain thing."* They have ideas of a godless world where man is exalted as god. They resist what they perceive to be any restraint on them. The Bible says that their ideas are vain, or empty.

When we look at this second Psalm, we have a picture of those without God speaking. When they speak, they speak to their own shame. When they speak, they imagine a vain thing. When they speak, their words are against God. Men and women apart from God have always spoken this way and they always will.

THE LORD SPEAKS

The Bible says in verse four, *"He that sitteth in the heavens shall laugh: The Lord shall have them in derision."* This second statement in this verse is a repetition of the first statement with more severity. *"Derision"* is using laughter as ridicule. The Bible says that God hears the lost lifting their voices against Him. He watches and listens as they want no restraint, no Bible, and no God.

Listening to many Christians, one would imagine that the world is out of control. However, from God's vantage point, He sits in heaven and laughs. He not only laughs, He ridicules them with laughter. He holds them in derision.

I cannot put myself in God's place, but I can understand what this psalm says as the world lifts its fist against God. The God who made that fist, and the mind who said to lift that fist, and the voice which enables that person to speak, and the ground on which that person stands, and the air which that person is breathing, and the nutrients in the earth which provide the food for the nourishment for that person to have strength to stand and say what he said, is laughing. Almighty God listens to that person speak, and the Bible says He laughs and holds them in derision.

The Bible says in verse five, *"Then shall he speak unto them in his wrath, and vex them in his sore displeasure."* God is going to speak to them in His wrath. He is going to vex them in His sore displeasure. They had their moment to speak, and now God says, "I am going to speak."

Do you remember the story of Esther? Do you remember wicked Haman who was going to rid the world of all the Jews? Do you remember the plan he concocted and the decree he got passed in order for the Persian king to make sure all the Jews were destroyed from the face of the earth? Do you remember the gallows he built for righteous Mordecai? Do you remember who rode through the streets in shame and who went to those gallows and died? It was not the Jews or Mordecai; it was wicked Haman who lifted his voice against God and God's people. We must never forget that God writes the last chapter!

> *We must never forget that God writes the last chapter!*

Often we hear only one side of the story. We hear the rage against God. We see the world lining up in rage against God. We hear all these immoral, indecent things that stir us up. We should be stirred up, but we should never forget that God still sits on the throne of the universe. The reins of the world remain in the hands of God. There is no need to worry, fear, or fret. God is in control.

As this psalm progresses in verse six, the Lord says, *"Yet have I set my king upon my holy hill of Zion."* The Lord says the kings of the earth have their plan, *"yet have I set my king upon my holy hill of Zion. I will declare the decree: the LORD hath said unto me, Thou art my Son; this day have I begotten thee."* This is a battle of kings with the King.

Speaking of the Lord Jesus, the Bible says in Hebrews 1:1-2, *"God, who at sundry times and in divers manners spake in time past unto the fathers by the prophets, hath in these last days spoken unto us by his Son, whom he hath appointed heir of all things, by whom also he made the worlds."*

God said that in time past He spoke through the prophets, but now He speaks through His Son, the Lord Jesus Christ. Keep this in mind as we look in the book of Isaiah. In Isaiah 9:6 the Bible says, *"For unto us a child is born, unto us a son is given: and the government shall be upon his shoulder: and his name shall be called Wonderful, Counsellor, The mighty God, The everlasting Father, The Prince of Peace."*

Remember that the lost speak and the Lord speaks. The Bible says that the Lord speaks through the Lord Jesus Christ. He says, *"I have set my king upon my holy hill of Zion."* He is talking about the Lord Jesus Christ.

The Bible says in Isaiah 9:6, *"Unto us a child is born..."* When Jesus Christ came to earth and was born in a manger, the wrath and rage of the world was against God. Wicked Herod the Great ordered all children the age of this babe born in Bethlehem to be murdered. What did God do? Herod died and the baby lived!

Friends, we are not losing this battle. The victory is ours. We have God's guarantee! We ought to have such confidence in God to know that all these things going on around us are not going to affect the plan of God or the outcome He has determined for our world.

Again in Isaiah 9:6 the Bible says, *"Unto us a son is given..."* When Jesus Christ went to Calvary, the Devil said, "This is it." In John 17, the Lord Jesus prayed in the garden of Gethsemane, *"The hour is come...I have finished the work which thou gavest me to do."* The victory was won there in the garden in prayer. When He went to Calvary, He cried out on the cross, *"It is finished."* He did not say, "I am finished," but *"It is finished."* From the world's perspective they said, "We have destroyed this Christ. We have gotten rid of Jesus. We don't have Him to deal with any longer." Men took His body down from the cross and buried it in a borrowed tomb.

In Romans 1:4 the Bible says, speaking of the Lord Jesus Christ, *"And declared to be the Son of God with power, according to the spirit of holiness, by the resurrection from the dead."* When the Son was given on Calvary, this raging, lost world lifted its fist to God. But the Bible says that it was God's plan for the Lord Jesus to die for our sin. On the third day He arose from the dead, alive forevermore.

At times we get caught in our thinking between His death and His resurrection. We behave like those frightened disciples closed up in a room because of fear. However, God has already proven that when Jesus Christ went to the cross and bled and died, and the world thought they had won the victory, they did not. The Bible says God spoke by His Son and raised Him from the dead, alive forevermore. This victory is ours in the Lord.

The kings of the earth are preparing to war an awful rage against the Son of God. In Revelation 13, the Bible tells us what the world is going to be like during the Tribulation period with the Antichrist and the False Prophet. Revelation 13:4 says, *"And they worshipped the dragon which gave power unto the beast: and they worshipped the beast, saying, Who is like unto the beast? who is able to make war with him?"*

If you read the twelfth and thirteenth chapters of the book of the Revelation of Jesus Christ, you find the rage of the Antichrist and the False Prophet. We find a world inflamed against God. There is a great building up for that very hour. However, all of this anti-God philosophy has not disturbed God one bit.

The Bible says in Revelation 14:1, *"And I looked, and lo, a Lamb stood on the mount Sion."* This Lamb is Jesus Christ. We call Psalm two a Messianic psalm because it is full of prophecy concerning our Messiah. Remember, verse two says, *"Yet have I set my king upon my holy hill of Zion."* Remember, Isaiah 9:6 says, *"...the government shall be upon his shoulder."*

This is established. This is settled forever. It is immovable. It is immutable. It is done. The Lord Jesus Christ shall reign.

LET US SPEAK

We must speak! In Psalm 2:8-9 the Bible says, *"Ask of me, and I shall give thee the heathen for thine inheritance, and the uttermost parts of the earth for thy possession. Thou shalt break them with a rod of iron; thou shalt dash them in pieces like a potter's vessel."*

That broken potter's vessel cannot be put back together. *"Be wise now therefore, O ye kings: be instructed, ye judges of the earth. Serve the LORD with fear, and rejoice with trembling. Kiss the Son..."*

This is one of God's great invitations. Man can be reconciled to God. This is done through His work on Calvary. *"Kiss the Son, lest he be angry, and ye perish from the way, when his wrath is kindled but a little. Blessed are all they that put their trust in him."*

In dealing with this psalm, I want you to hear the lost speak, I want you to hear the Lord speak, and I want you to recognize that those of us who know the Lord must speak. *"They"* in this last verse includes all true believers, all who have put their trust in Him.

We are living in a very unusual day. We are approaching the coming of Christ. We are nearer than any other generation to His return.

In the book of Acts, the early church took a strong stand for God. By the way, when you decide you are going to be strong for the Lord, the Devil is going to go into a rage. His disciples had been threatened and were told never to preach again in the name of Jesus Christ. What did they do? Let us see the account in Acts 4:23-29,

> *And being let go, they went to their own company, and reported all that the chief priests and elders had said unto them. And when they heard that, they lifted up their voice to God with one accord, and said, Lord, thou art God, which hast made heaven, and earth, and the sea, and all that in them is: who by the mouth of thy servant David has said, Why did the heathen rage, and the people imagine vain things? The kings of the earth stood up, and the rulers were gathered together against the Lord, and against his Christ. For of a truth against thy holy child Jesus, whom thou hast anointed, both Herod, and Pontius Pilate, with the Gentiles, and the people of Israel, were gathered together, for to do whatsoever thy hand and thy counsel determined before to be done. And now, Lord, behold their threatenings: and grant unto thy servants, that with all boldness they may speak thy word.*

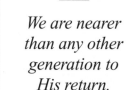

We are nearer than any other generation to His return.

When the disciples of our Lord were threatened because of their stand for God, they went right back to the second Psalm to find comfort. They said, "This is the way unbelievers always behave.

They lifted up their hand against God's Son and crucified Him on Calvary. This is the way they have always acted, and it is never going to be any different. It will never be any different until the Lord Jesus comes in glory." May our prayer be, "Lord, help us do this one thing–while the wicked are raging, help us to speak Your Word with holy boldness." This is a time for boldness!

We must not become so distracted by the raging of unbelievers that we forget that God has already set His Son on His holy hill of Zion. While they are speaking against Him, let us lift our voices for His glory. The greatest thing we can do in this hour of human history is to have a bold testimony for Jesus Christ. This is a time for courage and compassion. Rise up! Speak up!

Psalm 3

Lord, how are they increased that trouble me! many are they that rise up against me.

Many there be which say of my soul, There is no help for him in God. Selah.

But thou, O Lord, art a shield for me; my glory, and the lifter up of mine head.

I cried unto the Lord with my voice, and he heard me out of his holy hill. Selah.

I laid me down and slept; I awaked; for the Lord sustained me.

I will not be afraid of ten thousands of people, that have set themselves against me round about.

Arise, O Lord; save me, O my God: for thou hast smitten all mine enemies upon the cheek bone; thou hast broken the teeth of the ungodly.

Salvation belongeth unto the Lord: thy blessing is upon thy people. Selah.

CHAPTER
THREE

THE LORD SUSTAINED ME

 avid had committed a great sin with Bathsheba. His life was never the same after this. The sword never left his home and never left his heart. Though God forgave him and cleansed him as he sought the Lord, he had to deal with the consequences of his sinful behavior.

His son, Absalom, rebelled against him and sought to take his kingdom from him. There is no trouble on earth like trouble in your home. There is no joy and beauty on earth like a family working together and moving forward for God. David wrote the third Psalm while he was fleeing from his son Absalom. Psalm 3:1-8 says,

> *Lord, how are they increased that trouble me! many are they that rise up against me. Many there be which say of my soul, There is no help for him in God. Selah. But thou, O Lord, art a shield for me; my glory, and the lifter up of mine head. I cried unto the Lord with my voice, and he heard me out of his holy hill. Selah. I laid me down and slept; I awaked; for the Lord sustained*

me. I will not be afraid of ten thousands of people, that have set themselves against me round about. Arise, O LORD; save me, O my God: for thou hast smitten all mine enemies upon the cheek bone; thou hast broken the teeth of the ungodly. Salvation belongeth unto the LORD: thy blessing is upon thy people. Selah.

The Bible says in verse five, *"The LORD sustained me."* This would be a great statement for all of life. *"The LORD sustained me."* In other words, I could not have lived through it had not God provided what I needed.

This expression reminds me of another story found in the book of I Kings in the nineteenth chapter. The prophet Elijah had won a great victory for the Lord on Mount Carmel. The false prophets had been defeated, and Queen Jezebel was stirred up. She vowed to kill Elijah. The Word of God says that this mighty man of God, who had faced all those evil foes on Mount Carmel, ran for his life, trying to escape the wrath of Jezebel.

Elijah came to a certain place, sat under a juniper tree and prayed that he would die. God nourished him and gave him rest, allowed him to sleep, and fed him at the hands of an angel. In I Kings 19:7, the Lord told him, *"The journey is too great for thee."* We must all have the Lord's help. There is absolutely no way to be victorious without God's help.

Psalm three has eight verses. In these eight verses we find four divisions: verses one and two, verses three and four, verses five and six, and then verses seven and eight. These four parts make the whole.

DAVID'S PROBLEM

The psalmist cries out to the Lord in verses one and two, *"LORD, how are they increased that trouble me! many are they that rise up against me. Many there be which say of my soul, There is no help for him in God. Selah."*

We do not know exactly what that word *"selah"* means. We imagine it to be a pause, a time to stop and reflect about what is said. Seventy-three times it is used in the book of Psalms and three times in the book of Habakkuk.

When David considered the thought God gave him in verses one and two, he stopped to think about it. Notice what he is stopping to think about. *"Lord, how are they increased that trouble me!"* In other words, my problem is not getting smaller; it is getting bigger. My adversaries are not fewer; they are increasing.

Then he says, *"Many are they that rise up against me. Many there be which say of my soul, There is no help for him in God."*

Often things must get worse before they get better. We give our burdens to God when they become too great for us. Some of our heaviest burdens in life come as a result of failures in the home. Many Christian families never pray together in their home, never eat a meal

Could it be that God allowed this rebellion with Absalom, not only so David would have to deal with Absalom, but so that David would find that all he needed was in the Lord?

together, never offer thanks to God together at the table. I find it hard to believe that a Christian family would allow a television in a child's bedroom and allow that child to watch the television at will and see what they want to see behind closed doors. It takes more than saying that you are a Christian to have a Christian home. There are many people who are Christians who do not have a Christian home. There are many people who give a clear testimony and say, "I've asked God to forgive my sin, and by faith I've received Jesus Christ as my Savior," but do not have a Christian home. May God help us to desire to have a Christian home.

There is nothing so beautiful and so wonderful on the face of the earth as a family moving forward and working together for God. Nothing hurts so deeply as a family pulling apart–one part of that family moving toward God and the other part of that family going in the other direction.

David had a big problem on his hands and in his heart. His own son sought his life. His own son sought to overthrow the kingdom. To make bad matters worse, there is a sense in which David blamed himself for all of this because of the sin which he had committed.

David's chief counselor, Ahithophel, had also turned against him and had joined ranks with Absalom in his rebellion against King David. No wonder when Absalom was finally killed, David cried out in II Samuel 18:33, *"O my son Absalom, my son, my son Absalom! would God I had died for thee, O Absalom, my son, my son!"*

Someone has said David could have cried, "O, my sin, Absalom, my sin, my sin! Absalom, would God I had died for thee, O Absalom, my sin, my sin!"

David said, *"Many are they that rise up against me."* He was thinking of one in particular who was leading the rebellion, his own son. They were saying he had no right to ask God to help him. His enemies were tormenting him with criticism. There comes a time during a crisis when a man must know in his own heart that he has truly turned his heart toward God and has no merit of his own on which to seek the Lord, but he seeks the Lord for mercy on the merit of Jesus Christ.

He knows that God loves him and knows all about his trouble, all about his problems, all about his sorrow, and he seeks God's face. We are not going to live without difficulty. I am not going to live without difficulties, problems, and heartaches, many of which

38

I bring upon myself. You are not going to live without experiencing some rebellion, some people turning against you. Take hold of this truth, *"The LORD sustained me."*

DAVID'S PRAYER

Notice in verses three and four, David's prayer. David said, *"But..."* Even though they were criticizing him, and some of the things were justifiable, David knew he had sought God's forgiveness. The Bible language is, *"But thou, O LORD, art a shield for me; my glory, and the lifter up of mine head."*

He says, *"O LORD, thou art a shield."* "They're attacking me. Thou *'art a shield.'* I have no glory; Thou art *'my glory.'* My head is hung low. Thou art *'the lifter up of mine head.'"* Could it be that God allowed this rebellion with Absalom, not only so David would have to deal with Absalom, but so that David would find that all he needed was in the Lord?

Often in my life, as I was going through something painful, I came to see through faith that God allowed it, not for the problem's sake, but so that I would seek His face and find that all I need is in the Lord.

Whatever you are dealing with in life, have you turned the corner? Why did God allow this in your life? Why did God put this in your path? Why has this come to you? Why is it that you see other people who do not have these kinds of things to deal with? The Devil whispers, "God isn't as good to you as He is to them." The truth of the matter is, in your sorrow and in your problems, you are finding out more about the Lord and His goodness. You are seeing how sweet, how precious the Lord truly is. You are going deeper with God than you have ever gone.

David says, *"I cried unto the LORD with my voice."* That sounds a little strange, does it not? He could have said, "I cried unto the

Lord," but he said, *"I cried unto the LORD with my voice."* He used his voice to cry out to God. In other words, this was not a silent prayer. Sometimes we pray silently. Sometimes we pray aloud.

He says, *"I cried unto the LORD with my voice."* David wants us to know, "I raised my voice. I lifted up my voice. I cried out. I could not contain it. I could not simply think and speak silently with my heart to God. I raised my voice; my heart broke with sorrow, and I cried with my voice, *'and he heard me out of His holy hill.'"*

> There are many people who cannot get one good night's rest because they need spiritual cleansing and communion with Christ.

David said, "God answered me!" The Bible says in Hebrews 11:6, *"For he that cometh to God must believe that he is, and that he is a rewarder of them that diligently seek him."*

If all you see is the problem, and that problem does not cause you to seek God, then your life is constantly weighted down. Your burden is so heavy that you cannot live. There is no joy. God uses these things to help us realize on a daily basis that we need Him and that we can trust Him. We can walk with Him and we can cling to Him. He alone can hear and answer our prayers. As the burden grows greater, He proves again and again that His grace is sufficient. The Bible says in these verses that David prayed and the Lord heard him out of His holy hill.

DAVID'S PEACE

David found peace in the Lord. In verse five David says, *"I laid me down and slept; I awaked; for the LORD sustained me."* He not only slept, God gave him peace to sleep. He is not sleeping in the comfort of his palace. He is sleeping somewhere out in the open air with the stars and the sky as a canopy. He says, "God gave me such a peace in trusting Him, though many have risen against me. They seek my life. They say of me, 'It is not good for you to seek God because God is not going to help a sinner like you.' But I found something in the Lord that has given me peace in my soul. I can lay my head down in the wilderness and sleep and leave it all in God's hands."

Then the Lord calls him to wake. Why? The Lord *"sustained"* him. He kept him alive. David said to himself, no doubt, "I'm a man of war. I can take on any man. King Saul said to me one day, 'Why don't you kill some Philistines for my daughter?' I went out and killed twice as many as he thought I would have killed for his daughter. I'm the fellow who walked down in the valley and fought Goliath when the rest of the cowards sat on the hillside and didn't have the faith to trust God. I can match might with any man. I'm a warrior. I can hold my own. I've killed a bear; I've killed a lion."

A man believes that he is powerful and strong and able. We get the idea that God wants our weaknesses. No! God wants our strengths, not just our weaknesses. David said, "This is the strongest part of my life. I feel like I can stand man to man with anybody. I can defend myself against anyone, but in the strongest area of my life, God has brought me down to where I realize that I can't help myself, I can't save myself, I can't protect myself. All I can do is trust in God. He has sustained me and given me such peace that I can sleep, and I wake up because the Lord took care of me." This is beautiful.

There are many people who cannot rest because they are not right with God. There are many people who cannot get one good night's rest because they need spiritual cleansing and communion with Christ.

David had peace. Verses five and six say, *"I laid me down and slept; I awaked; for the LORD sustained me. I will not be afraid of ten thousands of people, that have set themselves against me round about."* He said, "I could be encircled by tens of thousands of people,

41

and I'm not going to fear because I know that God will take care of me." This is real peace.

There are great needs in every life, great needs in every family, great needs in every ministry, great needs in every business. But we can trust our great God who is greater than all our need.

I thought many times when rearing my children that they should do certain things. God said to me, "Why don't you take the first spiritual action? Why don't you trust Me? Why don't you lean on Me?" I found myself on my knees praying, "Dear God, touch my children. Dear God, help my home. Dear God, help me with this, that, and the other. Lord, work in our lives."

David wanted Absalom to get right with God. David said, "Whether he gets right or not, I'm getting right with God." God gave him peace. He could rest.

DAVID'S PROTECTION

In this psalm we find David's problem, David's prayer, David's peace, and David's protection. He says in verse seven, *"Arise, O LORD; save me, O my God: for thou hast smitten all mine enemies upon the cheek bone."* He is referring to his enemies as if they were wild beasts ready to pounce on him and devour him. He says, "You have broken their jaws. They can growl; they can scurry around and try to frighten me all they want to; but God has broken their jaws. Their jaws will not work. They are powerless to devour me."

Not only has God broken their jaws, he says, *"Thou hast broken the teeth of the ungodly."* God has broken their teeth. Their jaws are broken and their teeth are gone.

We live in a generation that is hateful toward the things of God. If you are not awake to this, you ought to be. This world is waging war against God. Many of God's children are sitting by and doing nothing.

The Bible says in Proverbs 30:11-14,

> *There is a generation that curseth their father, and doth not bless their mother. There is a generation that are pure in their own eyes, and yet is not washed from their filthiness. There is a generation, O how lofty are their eyes! and their eyelids are lifted up. There is a generation, whose teeth are as swords, and their jaw teeth as knives, to devour the poor from off the earth, and the needy from among men.*

The Bible says that this generation curses their father and does not bless their mother. They are lofty in their own eyes and their eyelids are lifted up. Their teeth are as swords: *"Whose teeth are as swords, and their jaw teeth as knives, to devour the poor from off the earth, and the needy from among men."* This is the kind of generation we have today. They want to bite and gnaw at the things of God and people who are trying to live for God.

Have you ever learned that friendship with the world is enmity with God? We are to win the lost to Christ, but not participate in their deeds. They are against everything godly and holy. David said, "They've raised up against me, but God has broken their jaws and removed their teeth."

Sometimes, even among God's people, this fighting and clawing goes on. Galatians 5:15 says, *"But if ye bite and devour one another, take heed that ye be not consumed one of another."* God says you bite and devour one another, and before long you are going to eat one another up entirely.

Many a man has been critical of his pastor and later needed his pastor to help his sons and daughters. Many a mother has bitten and devoured the spiritual leaders in the church and then did not have

43

them to help her son or daughter later in life. You need to be careful about biting, devouring, and consuming. Many parents have bitten and devoured a Christian teacher that their child had and then later needed that teacher to encourage their child.

> *The test of a man's spirituality is not in how he acts but in how he reacts.*

If you are the one that is being bitten and someone is trying to devour you, it is a great temptation to bite back. The test of a man's spirituality is not in how he acts but in how he reacts. Either we trust God or we do not trust God. Either we lean on the Lord or do not lean on the Lord. David did not want to kill his son. As a matter of fact, he said to his leaders, "When you have to deal with Absalom, for my sake, please deal kindly with my son."

David said, "God has given me the grace to trust Him." Have you trusted the Lord? He said, "God will protect me." Then he says in Psalm 3:8, *"Salvation belongeth unto the LORD."*

This sums it all up, but I think what David was saying was that there was nothing he could do to deliver himself. It is all of God. *"Salvation belongeth unto the LORD: thy blessing is upon thy people."* In other words, it is all in God's hands–all of it.

I think the statement in verse five sums up the entire Psalm, *"The LORD sustained me."* He gave me what I needed to get me through. Friend, He will give you what you need to get through any situation. There are no limitations to what God can get you through. There are no big jobs for God. No matter how great your need is, He will sustain you. Trust Him. Look to the Lord Jesus Christ at this moment!

PSALM 4

Hear me when I call, O God of my righteousness: thou hast enlarged me when I was in distress; have mercy upon me, and hear my prayer.

O ye sons of men, how long will ye turn my glory into shame? how long will ye love vanity, and seek after leasing? Selah.

But know that the LORD hath set apart him that is godly for himself: the LORD will hear when I call unto him.

Stand in awe, and sin not: commune with your own heart upon your bed, and be still. Selah.

Offer the sacrifices of righteousness, and put your trust in the LORD.

There be many that say, Who will shew us any good? LORD, lift thou up the light of thy countenance upon us.

Thou hast put gladness in my heart, more than in the time that their corn and their wine increased.

I will both lay me down in peace, and sleep: for thou, LORD, only makest me dwell in safety.

CHAPTER
FOUR

WHEN THE LORD ENLARGES US

hen we come to the fourth Psalm, we read the Word of God as it is given through a man who had his heart enlarged by the Lord. It costs something to have a big heart. As David cries out in this psalm, the Bible says in Psalm 4:1, *"Hear me when I call, O God of my righteousness: thou hast enlarged me when I was in distress; have mercy upon me, and hear my prayer."*

David spoke of a work God did in his life that gave him a greater capacity to care about the Lord and about the things of the Lord.

THE POSSIBILITY OF BEING ENLARGED BY THE LORD

Our God is able to work in our lives and make of us people who are more Christ-like, thus more caring and more compassionate. He can make us more able to express our concerns for the hurts and needs of others.

A lady came to my wife one day and said, "I want you to teach me how to care for people like you care for people. Teach me how to show compassion." I am sure that my wife shared with her some things that have taken place in her life that have enabled her to show compassion. This was a genuine request, but it required much more than an expression for an answer.

> *If God is to do the work in our lives that He desires to do, we must speak first to God before we speak to men.*

The key to this is right in the very beginning of this psalm. Notice that David says, *"Hear me when I call, O God of my righteousness."* Then in verse two, he says, *"O ye sons of men."* If God is to do the work in our lives that He desires to do, we must speak first to God before we speak to men. Of all the lessons we must learn, this is one of the most difficult.

I made a covenant with my wife, and I am trying to keep it. I should never complain at all, but I made a covenant that I would not complain about something that I had not prayed about. Instead of griping about it, I would not open my mouth about it unless I had prayed about it. I have discovered that when I start praying about these things, it becomes increasingly difficult to complain about them.

We should also determine that we will not speak to anyone about some difficulty or about anyone and their difficulty until first we talk to God about that person and the need. David cries out to God in this psalm, *"Hear me when I call, O God of my righteousness."*

He speaks to God before he speaks to men. There have been so many times in my life that I would not have spoken to men or about men if I had first spoken with God. As I think of this, my heart is convicted about the fact that I have talked too much and prayed too little. I have said too much about people before I said anything to God about those people.

THE PEOPLE GOD ENLARGES

The Lord works in and through the lives of people. Trust Him as your personal Savior and allow Him to enlarge your life. The Bible says, *"Hear me when I call, O God of my righteousness: thou hast enlarged me when I was in distress; have mercy upon me, and hear my prayer."*

In this psalm we learn that God enlarges people; He does not enlarge ministries. I have tried so many times in my life to build a bigger ministry, but what God wants to do is enlarge me. I have tried so many times in my life to extend the ministry, but what God desires to do is extend me. Does it shock you to think that God's chief interest is in the individual? As we are busy making plans, talking about what we can do to get more done, God is desiring all the while to get us to see that what He wants to do first in our lives.

I have talked too much and prayed too little. I have said too much about people before I said anything to God about those people.

If you have a pastor, a Sunday School teacher, or a soul winner with a big heart, the ministry will take care of itself. It is God who enlarges the heart.

The Lord does His work through people. When the Lord wants to do something, He finds someone He can work through to get it done. We place too much emphasis on the external and the material. David did not cry out, "Lord, give me a kingdom," or "Lord, give me a throne." He spoke of the fact that God had enlarged him.

As far as I am concerned, the main work God wants to do for me is the work He desires to do in me in this ministry. God desires to do a work in you as well.

THE PATHWAY TO BEING ENLARGED

The pathway to being enlarged is not a pathway we would choose for ourselves. I do not like this path. It goes against my nature. I do not want to deal with it or admit it, but it is in the Bible and I need to face it. The Bible says, *"Hear me when I call, O God of my righteousness: thou hast enlarged me when I was in distress."*

God uses distress to enlarge us. If you are a mature Christian, it is because you have had to deal with some distressing things. We all want to be mature Christians, at least we say we do; but we do not want to go through what is necessary to grow. Trouble borne in the spirit of Jesus Christ does not destroy people; it builds people.

You may be thinking about something that has gone on in your life with someone you love. It may have been the darkest hour you ever lived through; but in that hour you called out to God, and God did something in your heart that gave you a greater capacity for God and for the things of God. If it had never happened, God could never have enlarged you. It may have been sickness. It may have been disappointment. It may have been problems in the home. It may have been some difficulty in the church. Trouble borne in the spirit of Jesus Christ is the thing God uses in our lives to enlarge our hearts.

David said, "When I was distressed, when I was in a position where there was absolutely no way out, when I was being pressed from all sides and there was no hope, that is when God enlarged me."

There are many people who have walked in the valley of the shadow of death who can put their arm around others who are going through that valley and comfort them. There are many people who have been brokenhearted over their children who can be compassionate toward other people whose hearts are breaking over their children. There are many women who have borne pain and disappointment who can be a blessing and encouragement, because in that pain and disappointment they took it to the Lord Jesus, and He taught them that His grace is sufficient. This is not a matter of simply having trouble and heartache. It is what we learn about God and His comforting presence that we can share with others. God's Word says in II Corinthians 1:3-4, *"Blessed be God, even the Father of our Lord Jesus Christ, the Father of mercies, and the God of all comfort; who comforteth us in all our tribulation, that we may be able to comfort them which are in any trouble, by the comfort wherewith we ourselves are comforted of God."* This is not about boasting in your ability to get through a difficult situation; this is about giving God the glory for getting you through and telling others that the same God can get them through.

> *In this psalm we learn that God enlarges people; He does not enlarge ministries.*

God is not attempting to destroy us when we get into distressing situations. Just the opposite is true. God is building us. In your distresses you can think your life is over, or you and I can realize God wants to come to us and enlarge us in our distress. He gets us into a corner and begins working on us.

This happens in the life and ministry of a church. If churches are pastor-led, then what God must do to take the ministry a step further is enlarge the heart of the pastor. It is significant that David prays, *"Have mercy on me."* We all must come to the realization of needing

51

mercy because we get the idea that because we have served the Lord, we deserve His blessings.

He says in verse two, *"O ye sons of men, how long will ye turn my glory into shame? how long will ye love vanity, and seek after leasing? Selah."*

> *Trouble borne in the spirit of Jesus Christ does not destroy people; it builds people.*

"Leasing" is an old English word for lying. Men seek what they love. If you can tell me what you are trying to get, I can tell you what you love. If you love God, you will seek God. If you love money, you will seek money.

The Bible says in verse three, *"But know that the LORD hath set apart him that is godly for himself."* This is a blessed thing. Those of us who are saved and who love the Lord have been set apart. He has sanctified us. He has set us apart for Himself. We belong to the Lord. *"The LORD will hear when I call unto him."*

When I am in a tight place and do not know what to do, I want to open my mouth and start talking. I want to blame someone or something, but God says in verse four, *"Stand in awe."* Look to God. Stand still and be quiet. Listen.

Our Lord does not want us to stand in awe of our distress, but in awe of the greatness of our God. When you cannot get anything done, you find that what is most important is that God is greater than whatever you are facing. God says, "Don't talk. Stand in awe, and sin not." It is so easy to sin. Ephesians 4:26 says, *"Be ye angry, and sin not."*

There is a difference in controlled anger and uncontrolled anger. Controlled anger is directed at something you need to be angry about, and it is kept under control. There are some things going on in this world that should anger us. There are some things your children may do that you should be angry about. *"Be ye angry, and sin not"* means that you do not let the anger take over. You are not carried away by your anger. God says, "Stand in awe, and sin not." We are to be in awe before the Lord and to be quiet. The verse continues, *"Commune with your own heart upon your bed, and be still. Selah."* The word *"selah"* is a pause. So many times in my life my wife has kept me from the phone by saying, "Don't make that call tonight while you feel the way you do. Make it in the morning." The strangest thing happens. The next morning, I don't usually want to make the call. Do you ever get worked up and say, "I know what I am doing. Don't tell me what to do"? God says, *"Stand in awe, and sin not: commune with your own heart upon your bed, and be still. Selah."*

God wants us to wait on Him. When we do, we will not go out and make a fool of ourselves and bring reproach to the name of God. God is trying to work on us. Do you know what we must do? The Bible says in verse five, *"Offer the sacrifices of righteousness, and put your trust in the LORD."*

What does God want? He wants the sacrifices of righteousness. He wants us to depend on the Lord Jesus Christ. He wants us to lean on Him and trust in Him. Verse six says, *"There be many that say, Who will shew us any good? LORD, lift thou up the light of thy countenance upon us."*

> *Men seek what they love. If you can tell me what you are trying to get, I can tell you what you love. If you love God, you will seek God.*

We should say, "Show us, Lord. We are waiting on you. We are quiet. We are standing in awe. We are sinning not. We are communing with our own heart. We are shut up with You. Now turn the heavenly light on and show us Your way." This is the way God wants us to work. This is the pathway to being enlarged.

At times, I get started on this path, and then I jump off. I find myself in some distress, and I start trying to talk or work my way out of it. God says, "You didn't stay on the path. You were supposed to *'stand in awe, and sin not.'* You were supposed to *'commune with your own heart'* and wait on Me." There is a time to work hard, to put forth your best effort, but this comes after God has given you direction.

THE PEACE FROM THE ENLARGED LIFE

The Bible says in verses seven and eight, *"Thou hast put gladness in my heart, more than in the time that their corn and their wine increased. I will both lay me down in peace and sleep: for thou, Lord, only makest me dwell in safety."*

> *God wants us to wait on Him. When we do, we will not go out and make a fool of ourselves and bring reproach to the name of God.*

The Lord declares, "If you follow Me, the gladness I will put in your heart will far exceed what the world can offer."

Then He states that He gives peace. Do I know all the answers? No, but in the distress God taught me to trust Him, and in trusting Him, He gives me peace.

Some of you are worried about your kids. You wonder what they are going to do and who they are going to marry. You must come to the place where you can say, "I want God's will." We will have peace when we give it all to Jesus Christ. There is peace in placing faith in the Lord.

Be careful what you take into your heart. It will rob you of your sleep. It will rob you of peace. When you give things to God, He gives you peace from trusting Him.

David knew what this peace was like. When David was hiding in the wilderness, before he came to the throne, at times as many as three thousand of Saul's men were in pursuit of him. Can you imagine what God taught David at that time in his life? David learned that he could find a spot in the wilderness, stretch out under the stars, and know that God was going to take care of him. No one was going to surprise him in the night. Nothing was going to harm him. He could lie down like a baby and go to sleep with the peace of God in his heart. The only way we can have peace is to give all to the Lord.

The Lord is not finished with us. Do you know how I know this to be true? Because we are still here. Sometimes we get so weary that we feel there is nothing left for us. God is not finished, because we are still here. This is the way the Lord works.

We must put God before men. We must realize that God enlarges people, not ministries. The path to being enlarged involves distress, but through trusting Him in our distress, God brings us peace. Seek Him and discover the peace only He can give.

Psalm 5:7-12

But as for me, I will come into thy house in the multitude of thy mercy: and in thy fear will I worship toward thy holy temple.

Lead me, O Lord, in thy righteousness because of mine enemies; make thy way straight before my face.

For there is no faithfulness in their mouth; their inward part is very wickedness; their throat is an open sepulchre; they flatter with their tongue.

Destroy thou them, O God; let them fall by their own counsels; cast them out in the multitude of their transgressions; for they have rebelled against thee.

But let all those that put their trust in thee rejoice: let them ever shout for joy, because thou defendest them: let them also that love thy name be joyful in thee.

For thou, Lord, wilt bless the righteous; with favour wilt thou compass him as with a shield.

 LEAD ME, O LORD

 n the fifth Psalm, David prays for divine direction. He says in verse eight, *"Lead me, O LORD."* This is his prayer. Can you say from your heart that you desire divine direction? Are you willing to place the reins of your life in the hands of God and let Him take you where He pleases? *"Lead me, O LORD."* The Lord provides direction for all who will trust Him.

He is our Creator. If you have trusted Him as your Savior, He is your Redeemer, and you can say, *"Lead me, O LORD."*

In this psalm, there are twelve verses. There are two natural divisions, the first in verses one through seven, and the second beginning with verse eight through the end of the psalm. There is a weaving here. It is first to the believer in verses one, two, and three. There is a warning about the wicked in verses four, five, and six. Then it comes back to the believer in verses seven and eight, then back to the wicked in verses nine and ten, and then back to the believer in verses eleven and twelve. In the opening three verses the

57

believer is spoken of in the singular, then collectively spoken of in the plural in verses eleven and twelve.

THE LORD'S LEADING IS PERSONAL

This is a psalm about the life of a believer. Every believer's life should be a God-led life. The Lord's leadership is always personal. Make note of the personal pronouns in this passage. We read in verses one through three, *"Give ear to my words, O LORD; consider my meditation. Hearken unto the voice of my cry, my King, and my God: for unto thee will I pray. My voice shalt thou hear in the morning, O LORD; in the morning will I direct my prayer unto thee, and will look up."*

Are you willing to place the reins of your life in the hands of God and let Him take you where He pleases?

Again and again he says, *"my* words, *my* meditation, *my* cry, *my* King, *my* God, *I* pray, *my* voice, *I* direct, *my* prayer." The Lord's leading is always personal.

Often I say as a pastor that I want the Lord to lead our church, but there is a way in which God leads the church. He gives directions to individuals who have the responsibility of leadership in our church. Then He confirms that leadership in the hearts of people who are willing to follow the Lord's leadership. It is a personal matter.

There was a time in my life when someone shared with me the truth that I was a sinner, that if I died in my sins I would not go to heaven, and that Jesus Christ died for me. He paid my sin debt on the cross. He paid all of my debt. As the song writer who wrote "It Is Well With My Soul" said, "My sin–not in part, but the whole–was nailed to the cross and I bear it no more." The Lord Jesus paid my debt in full. He tasted death for every man. He was buried and He rose again bodily from the grave alive forevermore. When we ask Him to forgive our sin and by faith receive Him as Savior, the Lord Himself promised to hear our prayer, forgive our sin, and come to live in us.

I was born once physically. When I was born physically, God gave me certain abilities. He gave me a certain personality with my physical birth. Now I have experienced a spiritual birth. When I asked the Lord to forgive my sin and by faith trusted Christ as Savior, the Lord Jesus gave me spiritual gifts just as He gave others spiritual gifts when they were born into His family. Christ lives in me and desires to direct my life.

Since the Holy Spirit came to indwell me, He can impress upon me things I should do. God speaks to us through His Word. God speaks to us through other Christians. God speaks to us through circumstances.

I cannot say that every decision I have made has been a God-led decision, but I can say that as I sought God's guidance, He provided it. Our Lord declares in Psalm 32:8, *"I will guide thee."* I remember as an eighth grade student, shortly after I came to know the Lord Jesus as my Savior, I had an impression in my heart that I should attend another school. God used a particular circumstance to speak to me. It was after I was saved and the Lord came to live in me that God gave an impression in my heart that I should attend another school.

> *Every believer's life should be a God-led life. The Lord's leadership is always personal.*

I was going into the ninth grade. My mother went with me to the new school, and we entered the principal's office. In that office, God worked in the principal's heart. He gave me favor with that man. He told my mother that day, "I'm going to help you raise this boy." He was a Christian. He asked my mother, "Do you have the responsibility of raising this boy by yourself?" She said, "Yes." He said, "I'm going to help you." At the time I did not know what that entailed, but I came to find out it meant quite a few things, including the "board of education."

Think about how many people are laboring for the Lord, but are not happy in the Lord. Activity must never become a substitute for true spirituality.

It was at that school that God revealed to me His will for my life. It was there that I met the girl I would marry. I cannot say to you that I knew at the moment that God was guiding me. I can say, looking back across the years that I was a saved person and it was a time in my life when I wanted to do what God wanted me to do, and I know now that God led me. I can see God's hand was in it.

The leadership of the Lord is a personal matter. I wonder at times if I am as sensitive to the leading of the Lord today as I was then. God desires to direct your life. This means that if you are a child of God, the Lord wants to lead you day by day in the path He desires for you. The leading of the Lord is a personal matter.

THE LORD'S LEADING IS PROVIDED

The Lord's leading is not only personal; it is provided. Many people say, "I don't know what to do." That is not God's fault. The Bible says in the first verse of this psalm, *"Give ear to my words."* In the first half of this psalm, the psalmist David speaks of his talk, and then, in the closing part, of his walk. Here he says, *"Give ear to my words, O LORD; consider my meditation."* In this particular context, meditation had to do with what David could not express in words.

The Bible says in Romans 8:26-27,

> *Likewise the Spirit also helpeth our infirmities: for we know not what we should pray for as we ought: but the Spirit itself maketh intercession for us with groanings which cannot be uttered. And he that searcheth the hearts knoweth what is the mind of the Spirit, because he maketh intercession for the saints according to the will of God.*

There are *"groanings which cannot be uttered."* There are times when we come to the Lord and our hearts are heavy and burdened, our words do not come easily. We cannot express our thoughts in sentence structure to the Lord. It is as though we do not know what figures of speech to use, but there is a yearning and groaning inside of us to know God and to have God help us. As we pray and meditate and groan before God, He will provide the leadership we need.

David says, *"O LORD, consider my meditation. Hearken unto the voice of my cry, my King, and my God: for unto thee will I pray."* The king of Israel needed "the King." The pastor needs a Pastor. Every father needs the heavenly Father. David, anointed king of Israel, said, "Lord, You are my King. I need my King."

"My voice shalt thou hear in the morning, O LORD; in the morning will I direct my prayer unto thee, and will look up." He did not say, "I will look out, I will look around, I will look down, or I will look in." All of us have problems. Sometimes the problem is looking in, being too introspective. Many times we torment ourselves over sins that have been forgiven. *"Look up"* to God.

When you start looking in, remember *"all things work together for good to them that love God, to them who are the called according to his purpose"* (Romans 8:28). God allows certain things in our lives that we have no choice in because He intends to conform us to the image of His Son, and it took that ingredient. When you start looking in too much, all that introspection can be discouraging. The psalmist did not say, "I look in." He did not say, "I look out." He did not look down. He said, *"I...will look up."*

Make special note of this statement in verse three, *"My voice shalt thou hear in the morning, O LORD."* George Mueller lived a century ago. He was an evangelist, a preacher, a missionary, and director of children's orphanages in England. He prayed in over eight million dollars without ever telling anyone any amount that he needed, without asking for it or sending a letter for it. He prayed in over eight million dollars for those orphans. A man like that has something to say to us.

> *You may be an informed Christian, without being a spiritually minded Christian.*

We have a record of how Mueller started each day. Let me give you a portion of his testimony. He said,

I saw more clearly than ever that the first great and primary business to which I ought to attend every day was to have my soul happy in the Lord.

The first thing to be concerned about was not how much I might serve the Lord or how I might glorify the Lord or how I might get my soul into a happy state, but how I might get my soul into a happy state and how my inner man might be nourished; for I might seek to set the truth before the unconverted. I might seek to benefit believers. I might seek to relieve the distressed. I might in other ways seek to behave myself as it becomes a child of God in this world, and yet, not being happy in the Lord, not being nourished and strengthened in my inner man day by day, all this might not be attended to in a right spirit.

In other words Mueller said, I might do all those things, but I will not have the right spirit about it. He continued in his testimony,

> Before this time my practice had been at least for ten years previously, as an habitual thing, to give myself to prayer after having dressed myself in the morning. Now I saw that the most important thing I had to do was to give myself to the reading of God's Word and to meditation on it that thus my heart might be comforted, encouraged, warmed, reproved, instructed, and that thus, by means of the Word of God while meditating on it, be brought into experiential communion with the Lord.

> I began therefore to meditate on the New Testament from the beginning, early in the morning. The first thing I did after having asked in a few words the Lord's blessing upon His precious Word, was to begin to meditate on the Word of God, searching as it were in every verse to get blessing out of it, not for the sake of the public ministry of the Word, not for the sake of preaching on what I had meditated upon, but for the sake of obtaining food for my own soul.

> The result I have found to be almost invariably this: that after a very few minutes my soul has been led to confession or to thanksgiving or to intercession or to supplication, so that I did not as it were give myself to prayer, but to meditation. Yet, it turned almost immediately more or less into prayer.

> When thus I have been for a while, making confession or intercession, supplication or have given thanks, I go to the next words or verse, turning all as I go on into prayer for myself or others, as the Word may

lead to it, but still continually keeping before me that
food for my own soul is the object of my meditation.

This man of God said, "For years, what I did is jump right into
prayer. I got myself dressed and began to pray." He said, "I learned,
after ten years, that this was not the best way. What I did was bring
myself into communion with God to make myself happy in the Lord
Jesus. Then prayer came out of that."

If we do not learn to take what God has provided, we are never
going to be happy in the Lord Jesus. Think about how many people
are laboring for the Lord, but are not happy in the Lord. I have been
told that one thousand Baptist preachers quit the ministry every
year. They say they are doing the grandest work in all the world, but
they cannot stand to do it any longer. Activity must never become a
substitute for true spirituality.

This is why George Mueller said, "I make myself happy in Jesus."
This is the same thing that God gave David to pen in Psalm 5. In
the morning let us meet the Lord. Let us meet the Lord with our
meditations. It is a matter of developing a devotional life and from
that devotional life walking in the ways of the Lord.

*"My voice shalt thou hear in the morning, O LORD; in the morning
will I direct my prayer unto thee, and will look up."* What will it take
to determine we are going to meet God in the morning? I want to
start the day like a rocket. I want to blast off every day. After blasting
off for years, it is difficult for me to find the fuel every day to take
off. I am not talking about physical energy. We need the strength that
only God can give.

The Lord has designed it so that early in life we can get the right
foundation. Do you still marvel as I do at how much a one-year-old,
two-year-old, or three-year-old can learn? Do you marvel at what
these children come up with? God has designed life so that when it
begins, the right foundation can be laid. God has designed marriage

so that when it begins, the right foundation can be placed in marriage. There are people, for example, who get married and do not have the right foundation. They just try to hang on to any bits or pieces they have gotten, and after five or ten years they still have no foundation.

Sunday is the first day of the week. We meet God, worship God, adore God, and look to God to guide us for the rest of the week. We need to adjust our thinking so that Sunday is not the last day of the week; it is the first day of the week. There must be something to closing the week on the seventh day, Saturday, resting in what has been done and finding a new beginning on Sunday.

If you have a marriage that did not get started right and you must uproot some things, it is very disturbing. Many people want to split up because they did not get the right foundation early in marriage. If you are going to get the foundation, you must uproot some things to make a place for the foundation that you did not get in the beginning.

> *At times He will make us wait on Him. It is not because He is late, but because we are early. We are not ready to receive His instruction.*

God has provided leadership. He waits for us every morning to ask Him for that leadership for the day, but often we do not meet Him. Eventually it catches up with us. It catches up with a marriage that has not been built on the right foundation.

I do not know your schedule. Perhaps you must get up at two o'clock in the morning and start your day, but there is a morning. Make it a priority and ask God to help you to meet Him in the morning. Ask the Lord for what is needed in order to "look to the Lord."

Deal with the television. There is not a spiritual man in the world who watches television late at night. There is no such thing as a

65

spiritual Christian who sits up late at night and watches television. You may be an informed Christian, without being a spiritually minded Christian.

Be careful about what you read before you go to bed at night. Do not allow every kind of garbage in the world to go through your eye gate and your ear gate. Listen to the right thing, look at the right thing, think about the right thing, because in the night hours God wants to minister to us so we can meet Him in the morning. God waits for us in the morning to provide leadership for the day.

THE LORD'S LEADING IS PLAIN

The Lord's leadership is personal; the Lord's leadership is provided; the Lord's leadership is also plain. Listen to David's prayer here in verse eight, *"Lead me, O LORD, in thy righteousness because of mine enemies; make thy way straight before my face."*

David talks about his enemies here in verses four, five, and six,

> *For thou art not a God that hath pleasure in wickedness: neither shall evil dwell with thee. The foolish shall not stand in thy sight: thou hatest all workers of iniquity. Thou shalt destroy them that speak leasing: the LORD will abhor the bloody and deceitful man.*

Then he says in verses seven and eight,

> *But as for me, I will come into thy house in the multitude of thy mercy: and in thy fear will I worship toward thy holy temple. Lead me, O LORD, in thy righteousness because of mine enemies; make thy way straight before my face.*

Remember that the word *"leasing"* is an old English word for *lying*. Many Christians will not admit to their lying, but they are full of guile. They do not tell it exactly like it is.

"Make thy way straight before my face." The Lord's leading is plain. Can someone who is a Christian know with certainty what it is that God wants him to do? Can a young man who is a Christian say, "I believe this is who God wants me to marry"? Certainly. Can a young lady who is a Christian say, "I know this is who God wants me to marry"? Can a young couple say with certainty, "I know this is what God wants us to do with our children"? Can a young family say, "This is where God wants us to worship Him in a church"? Sure. The Lord's leading is plain.

A wonderful prayer is found in Psalm 27:11, *"Teach me thy way, O LORD, and lead me in a plain path, because of mine enemies."*

This path is the path of His righteousness. *"Lead me, O LORD, in thy righteousness."* We can go to God and get the leadership we need.

At times He will make us wait on Him. It is not because He is late, but because we are early. We are not ready to receive His instruction.

I say to people often who talk to me about God's will, "Are you serious?" "Yes." "Are you a sincere Christian?" "Yes." "Do you want to know what God wants for you?" "Yes." Then I say, "Friend, you don't have a worry in the world. You don't have anything to fret about because in God's good time, He will provide exactly the leadership you need."

THE LORD'S LEADING IS PLEASANT

The Lord's leading is personal; it is provided; it is plain; it is also pleasant. His commandments are not grievous. The Lord's leading is pleasant, but the Bible says, *"The way of transgressors is hard"* (Proverbs 13:15). John Newton wrote, "Through many dangers, toils and snares I have already come." We have certainly come *through* many dangers, toils and snares. The song does not say, *"To* many dangers, toils and snares." The songwriter had it right. He said, *"Through* many dangers, toils and snares I have already come."

This is why the fifth Psalm weaves back and forth as it does. Here are the righteous; there are the wicked. The wicked are destroyed, but God takes the righteous right on through. His leading is pleasant. No wonder the Bible says in verse eleven, *"But let all those that put their trust in thee rejoice: let them ever shout for joy."*

We should shout and praise God more. There should be more emotion expressed by the children of God. We have in Christ *"joy unspeakable and full of glory."*

As the Lord works for you in the circumstances on your job, you should say, "Praise God! Look what the Lord did for me!" When somebody gives you a raise, say, "Thank the Lord Jesus! He's the One behind all this!"

God's people should be praising Him. The Bible says in verse eleven, *"Let them ever shout for joy, because thou defendest them: let them also that love thy name be joyful in thee."* This is what George Mueller was talking about. He got tired of starting the day trying to get an engine cranked that didn't want to crank. He came to the place where he was happy in Jesus Christ. He came into communion with Christ. He entered into fellowship with the Lord. He tasted of heavenly things until his appetite started increasing. Then he just started praying and God led him.

The Bible says in verse twelve, *"For thou, LORD, wilt bless the righteous; with favour wilt thou compass him as with a shield."*

We are not righteous. The Lord leads us in paths of righteousness. He has made us righteous by His imputed righteousness. He gives us favor.

"My Father is rich in houses and lands. He holdeth the wealth of the world in His hands. Of rubies and diamonds, of silver and gold, His coffers are full; He has riches untold. I'm a child of the King, a child of the King. With Jesus my Savior, I'm a child of the King."

The King is waiting to lead us through. The Lord is waiting in the morning to lead us through the day. He will be our guide through many dangers, toils and snares.

Let us pray as David did, *"Lead me, O LORD."*

Psalm 6

O Lord, rebuke me not in thine anger, neither chasten me in thy hot displeasure.

Have mercy upon me, O Lord; for I am weak: O Lord, heal me; for my bones are vexed.

My soul is also sore vexed: but thou, O Lord, how long?

Return, O Lord, deliver my soul: oh save me for thy mercies' sake.

For in death there is no remembrance of thee: in the grave who shall give thee thanks?

I am weary with my groaning; all the night make I my bed to swim; I water my couch with my tears.

Mine eye is consumed because of grief; it waxeth old because of all mine enemies.

Depart from me, all ye workers of iniquity; for the Lord hath heard the voice of my weeping.

The Lord hath heard my supplication; the Lord will receive my prayer.

Let all mine enemies be ashamed and sore vexed: let them return and be ashamed suddenly.

OUR GOD AND HIS CHILDREN

"FOR THY MERCIES' SAKE"

f the one hundred and fifty psalms, there are seven called the penitential psalms, psalms of the penitent. Psalm six is the first of these. The other penitential psalms are Psalm thirty-two, thirty-eight, fifty-one, one hundred and two, Psalm one hundred thirty, and Psalm one hundred forty-three. In Psalm six we look at the heart of God as He deals with the heart of one of His children. The Bible says in Psalm 6:1-10,

> *O LORD, rebuke me not in thine anger, neither chasten me in thy hot displeasure. Have mercy upon me, O LORD; for I am weak: O LORD, heal me; for my bones are vexed. My soul is also sore vexed: but thou, O LORD, how long? Return, O LORD, deliver my soul: oh save me for thy mercies' sake. For in death there is no remembrance of thee: in the grave who shall give thee thanks? I am weary with my groaning; all the night make I my bed to swim; I water my couch with*

my tears. Mine eye is consumed because of grief; it waxeth old because of all mine enemies. Depart from me, all ye workers of iniquity; for the LORD hath heard the voice of my weeping. The LORD hath heard my supplication; the LORD will receive my prayer. Let all mine enemies be ashamed and sore vexed: let them return and be ashamed suddenly.

Note a marvelous expression in the fourth verse of this sixth Psalm, where the psalmist declares, *"For thy mercies' sake."* How can we approach the Lord? How can sinful men approach a holy God? This can happen only because of His mercy.

One day I was at the church taking care of some things, and some of our little girls from the church were riding bicycles nearby. They saw me open the door, and suddenly they stopped and darted inside. It was not a "church day," it was not Sunday School time, the Christian school was not in operation, but they came in the door of the building. I asked, "What do you girls need today?" They replied, "We need a drink of water." They knew they could approach me and come into the building, and they had every right in the world to come inside and get what they needed. They had no hesitation at all. I am glad they felt that way. Recognizing me as the pastor and knowing I cared for them, they boldly entered in.

What right do sinful people have to approach a holy God? We are hard on sinners. At times, I think we are harder on sinners than God is. There is no doubt we have a "sin-hating" God, but never forget that He is a "sinner-loving" God. David cried out to the Lord and said, "I need deliverance and salvation for Thy mercies' sake." This is the only way to God. We come to God, not on our merit, but on His mercy. We cannot approach Him any other way.

Before taking a closer look at the sixth Psalm, let us recall a beautiful story given to us in the New Testament. In the eighteenth

chapter of the Gospel according to Luke, the Lord gives us this parable. In verses nine through fourteen the Bible says,

> *And he spake this parable unto certain which trusted in themselves that they were righteous, and despised others: two men went up into the temple to pray; the one a Pharisee, and the other a publican. The Pharisee stood and prayed thus with himself, God, I thank thee, that I am not as other men are, extortioners, unjust, adulterers, or even as this publican. I fast twice in the week, I give tithes of all that I possess. And the publican, standing afar off, would not lift up so much as his eyes unto heaven, but smote upon his breast, saying, God be merciful to me a sinner. I tell you, this man went down to his house justified rather than the other: for every one that exalteth himself shall be abased; and he that humbleth himself shall be exalted.*

The poor publican who recognized he was a sinner said, *"God, be merciful to me."* The word *"merciful"* here is connected with the mercy seat. If you remember, the mercy seat was part of the Ark of the Covenant, the small wooden box overlaid with gold, which had a golden lid. Inside one would find the Law on tables of stone. On that lid, at a special time, blood was applied. When the blood was sprinkled on the golden lid, the mercy seat, the Law could not speak through that golden lid with blood sprinkled on it. The blood covered the Law, and there was mercy to be found through the blood.

This poor sinner cried, "The mercy seat! I don't need justice. I need mercy! I recognize, Lord, that I deserve to die and go to hell forever, but I need mercy. Have mercy upon me. The mercy seat, Lord Jesus, is what I need."

We are so haughty. We live in a world of haughty people. We live in a world of proud people. There are some who think they are above sin and others who behold those who have sinned, who seem to declare by the way they look that they are incapable of doing what others have done. In truth, we are all sinners in need of the mercy of God.

THE CHASTENING OF THE BELIEVER

God be merciful to all of us. We all need mercy. David said, *"For thy mercies' sake."* Notice please in this sixth Psalm the chastening of the believer.

The psalmist says, *"O LORD, rebuke me not in thine anger, neither chasten me in thy hot displeasure."* Make special note of the words *"rebuke"* and *"chasten."* When the Lord deals with us, those of us who are His children, He deals with us with His Word and then with His rod. We have an opportunity to listen to His Word and not feel His rod. If we do not harken to His Word, we shall surely feel His rod. There is no way to escape it.

Take all the religions in the world and compare them with Christianity. Christianity is not a religion; it is life in Christ. But just to illustrate, let us place our Christian faith alongside other religions. We are going to find that people believe they can be saved from their sin one of two ways: either God saves men, or men save themselves.

The Bible teaches that God saves men. Men are lost in their sin and they need a Savior. They have no hope without Christ. The only thing that awaits sinful men is death and hell forever. The Lord Jesus suffered our death and hell for us. He paid our debt with His precious blood on the cross of Calvary. He bled and died, was buried, and rose triumphantly from the grave alive forevermore. Those who ask Him to forgive their sin and by faith receive Him as Savior have His full, free, and forever promise that their sins are forgiven and forgotten and cast behind God's back (Isaiah 38:17). Heaven is their home. This is based on no merit of their own, but entirely on the merit of the Lord Jesus Christ.

In this world we find two "children." There are those who are children of the Devil and those who are children of the Lord. We are children of the Devil by nature and must become children of God by faith in the Lord Jesus Christ. God does not chasten children of the Devil. He chastens only His children, those who have been born into His family by faith. When reading this psalm, we see that David had sinned, and evidently sickness had resulted from his sin. It appeared that the sickness could have led to death.

David said, "I know I am going to be rebuked. You are going to tell me when I am wrong. You are going to speak to me, but rebuke me not in thy anger. I know I am going to be chastened." The word *"chastened"* has to do with child training, disciplining, or getting back in line. David said, "I know that I am going to feel the chastening rod, but do not chasten me in Thy hot displeasure. I know that I am going to be chastened."

> *God is going to deal with His children until we deal with that sin.*

We are chastened as God's children when we are not willing to confess our sins and heed God's Word. If we think we can live in sin, we are wrong. God is going to deal with His children until we deal with that sin.

Let us consider two classic passages of Scripture in the New Testament concerning chastening. Look first at Hebrews 12:3-6,

> *For consider him that endured such contradiction of sinners against himself, lest ye be wearied and faint in your minds. Ye have not yet resisted unto blood, striving against sin. And ye have forgotten the exhortation which speaketh unto you as unto children, My son, despise not thou the chastening of the Lord, nor faint when thou art rebuked of him: for*

whom the Lord loveth he chasteneth, and scourgeth every son whom he receiveth.

God does not chasten unbelievers, because they are going to die and go to hell. Christians face nothing of that punishment after they leave this world. God's children are going to heaven. The Lord deals with His children in the here and now. The Bible says, *"He chasteneth, and scourgeth every son whom he receiveth. If ye endure chastening, God dealeth with you as with sons; for what son is he whom the father chasteneth not?"*

> *Your life does not have to end in darkness. The painful things you go through in life do not have to be the final act of life.*

If you can get by in your sin without being chastened, then you need to seriously think about whether or not you are truly a child of God. Many Christians have the idea that they are going to have to pay for their sin. Let us get the terminology straight. The Lord Jesus paid for all of our sin on the cross.

The songwriter Mr. Spafford had it right in his wonderful hymn, "It Is Well With My Soul." One verse states, "My sin–not in part, but the whole–is nailed to the cross and I bear it no more. Praise the Lord, praise the Lord, O my soul!" If you pay for sin, the payment of sin is death and hell. We are not going to pay for our sin in that sense. We are not going to go to hell. But if you are using the word *pay*, meaning you are going to be disciplined for sin as a father would discipline or chasten his child, this is correct. But it would be better not to use the word *pay*. Our sin was paid for, not in part but the whole, when the Lord Jesus died for our sin on the cross. He paid for all our sin–past, present, and future.

I am a child of God. Do you know what it means to be a child of God? It means I have a heavenly Father who deals with me as a child. To be chastened is an evidence of being a Christian.

David actually affirmed that he was a believer in Psalm six by acknowledging that he was going to be chastened. David said, "There is no doubt in my mind I am going to be rebuked. There is no doubt in my mind that I am going to be chastened because I know that I am a believer. I know that I am not going to go to hell, so I know that God is going to deal with me in the here and now." He had no doubt about his salvation.

Let us consider another passage in the New Testament concerning chastening. The passage is in I Corinthians chapter eleven. Concerning the memorial supper that our Lord left us, the Bible says in verses twenty-eight and twenty-nine, *"But let a man examine himself, and so let him eat of that bread, and drink of that cup. For he that eateth and drinketh unworthily..."* The word *"unworthily"* has to do with the manner in which we observe this memorial supper. We are all unworthy. But we are not to partake of this ordinance unworthily. *"For he that eateth and drinketh unworthily, eateth and drinketh damnation to himself, not discerning the Lord's body."* It is a very serious matter for a Christian to come to the Lord's table with unconfessed sin in his life. This brings God's chastening.

Paul then wrote to the church in Corinth explaining why so many of them were weak, why many were sick, and why some members had already died. They had not judged themselves. He says in verses thirty through thirty-two, *"For this cause many are weak and sickly among you, and many sleep. For if we would judge ourselves, we should not be judged. But when we are judged, we are chastened of the Lord, that we should not be condemned with the world."*

If a child of God can get by with sin, then the world looks on and says, "There is nothing different there." When we sin as believers, we have an opportunity to confess our sins. God uses His Word to rebuke us and convict us of our sin, and we are to confess our sin. If we do not confess our sin at that rebuke, God is going to chasten us.

Stop! We must also understand that not all suffering is because of sin. Sin is a serious matter. There is nothing playful about sin. There is only tragedy.

The Bible teaches very clearly that God chastens some people and they become weak physically. His chastening can lead to being sick physically. But not all sickness is because of the chastening of the Lord. You do not need to ask yourself every time something adverse happens, "What have I done wrong?" But God may use sickness for chastening. God speaks to His children to let them know the purpose for their suffering.

God may use premature death in chastening. In the sixth Psalm, we find David thinking, "Lord, am I going to die? I don't want to die. This is going to be a premature death. I know that chastening could be death, and I don't want this to happen." We can also experience the loss of the joy of our salvation. Psalm 51:12 says, *"Restore unto me the joy of thy salvation."*

One can lose wealth and property as a result of chastisement. Some people have it made–they do anything in the world, go anywhere they want to go, spend money on anything they want to, but they do not honor God, and they are God's children. They do not pay the tithe and give offerings to the work of the Lord. Why should God allow them be healthy and strong and flaunt their wealth and not honor Him, yet be one of His children? Do they not know God may deal with them and chasten them by removing property or wealth from them? The Bible teaches this. You may say, "What right does He have to do that?" He has the right of Calvary. He has the right of His shed blood. He can do as He pleases with His children.

Some people are chastened by the loss of loved ones. In chapter twelve of I Samuel God tells of David's baby boy being taken because of David's sin. It is a serious matter for a child of God not to deal

78

with his sin. If we are going to speak out like this about sin, let us also speak with compassion about His forgiveness.

THE CONSEQUENCES OF SIN

Notice the consequences of sin as we continue through this psalm. Verse two says, *"Have mercy upon me, O LORD; for I am weak."* We have just seen in I Corinthians chapter eleven that weakness is part of chastening. David said, *"I am weak."* Here he was, a strong man, a man who had killed a bear, who had killed a lion, who had fought and slain a giant, who had led an army. Now he says, *"I am weak." "O LORD, heal me; for my bones are vexed."* The word *"vexed"* means "to tremble inwardly." David declares, "The framework of my body is trembling inwardly. I am not the man I was. I feel it in my body." These are the consequences of his sin.

"My soul is also sore vexed." In our soul, we have intellect, emotion, and will. The soul informs the body. The body performs for the soul. At times people do things with their body that they should not do. As a result, they not only experience the chastisement of God in their bodies, but they experience the chastisement of God in their souls, because the soul informed the body. The one that *informs* and the one that *performs* both suffer the effects and consequences of sin.

The Bible continues, *"My soul is also sore vexed: but thou, O LORD, how long? Return, O LORD, deliver my soul: oh save me for thy mercies' sake."* Notice that it becomes even more frightening. *"For in death there is no remembrance of thee."* David asks, "Lord, am I going to die? Are You actually going to take my life?" *"In the grave who shall give thee thanks?"* As I mentioned before, some Christians do die prematurely because of their sin. I do not know when people cross that line, but I know that it happens.

I was speaking in a church where the people had been praying for a certain gentleman. He came to the service. They invited him to come to hear me preach. Before I went to the pulpit to preach, I sat down near the front of the church during the song service. The man sat close enough to me that I could reach out with my arm and touch him. I heard not long after that meeting, the man went to an abandoned building and took his own life. He did not answer any questions; he just created questions with suicide. That did not help anyone. Suicide is not an answer for anything. It is a selfish way to exit this world. Thousands of people in our country commit suicide every year. Some estimate as many as sixty thousand people every year commit suicide in America.

David said, "Lord, I don't want to die. I don't want to go out prematurely. I don't want to die." Think about the consequences of sin.

David said in verse six, *"I am weary."* He was a giant-killer, a lion-slayer, a bear-killer, an army leader, and a valiant warrior, yet he said, *"I am weary with my groaning; all the night make I my bed to swim; I water my couch with my tears. Mine eye is consumed because of grief."* I actually believe that his eyesight was affected. It is my belief that his eyesight was affected by this weariness and grief.

Some of us know that at times our vision becomes impaired from the pressure, the grief, and the burden. David said, "I feel this in my bones. I feel it in my body. I recognize this in my soul. I feel it in my eyes. *"It waxeth old because of all mine enemies."* He spoke of people who did not love him and did not care about him. All they did was rejoice over his condition.

So many people have lost the fear of God. Millions joke about God. Even many of God's children have lost the idea of the horribleness of sin. We are never going to have revival until we see the Lord *"high and lifted up"* and talk about a sin-hating God, not a sinner-hating God, and we name sin for the wickedness it really is.

THE CRY OF THIS SINNER

The Bible says in verse eight, *"Depart from me, all ye workers of iniquity; for the LORD hath heard the voice of my weeping."* This makes me want to shout. There is hope. Your life does not have to end in darkness. The painful things you go through in life do not have to be the final act of life.

The Devil says, "Come, join in. Have a good time. Get involved. Indulge yourself." You cross a barrier. It may not be much of a barrier for some people, but it is a mighty one for you. The world may say there is nothing to it. But as a Christian, God holds you to the highest standard. He does not hold the world to this same standard. Even among those who are in God's family, God holds certain people to a closer standard, because some have had so much opportunity.

First the Devil invites, then he becomes the accuser. He was a host, then he became a slanderer. He is a liar and a deceiver. He turns on you like the beast he really is and says, "This is your life. This is what has become of it. This is what you are. This is what you are going to always be." David said, "No, it is not. I cried to the Lord, and He heard my weeping. The Lord Jesus has heard me. And He is going to help me."

In verses eight through ten the Bible says,

> *Depart from me, all ye workers of iniquity; for the LORD hath heard the voice of my weeping. The LORD hath heard my supplication; the LORD will receive my prayer. Let all mine enemies be ashamed and sore vexed: let them return and be ashamed suddenly.*

The Lord God broke through. He has dealt with me. He has rebuked me and chastened me. I have dealt with my sin. I have confessed it to God. I have called on the Lord. He has heard my weeping. I cried out to God. He heard the voice of my weeping. Tears have a voice that God listens to attentively.

David says, "The Lord has come to me for His mercies' sake." God never deals with His children without the ultimate goal of bringing them to the place of restoration and usefulness again. This is what the Lord does. The Lord Jesus is a wonderful Savior. Tell the dirty Devil that only God knows the last chapter, and He is able to make it have a happy ending.

PSALM 7:1-10

O LORD my God, in thee do I put my trust: save me from all them that persecute me, and deliver me:

Lest he tear my soul like a lion, rending it in pieces, while there is none to deliver.

O LORD my God, if I have done this; if there be iniquity in my hands;

If I have rewarded evil unto him that was at peace with me; (yea, I have delivered him that without cause is mine enemy:)

Let the enemy persecute my soul, and take it; yea, let him tread down my life upon the earth, and lay mine honour in the dust. Selah.

Arise, O LORD, in thine anger, lift up thyself because of the rage of mine enemies: and awake for me to the judgment that thou hast commanded.

So shall the congregation of the people compass thee about: for their sakes therefore return thou on high.

The LORD shall judge the people: judge me, O LORD, according to my righteousness, and according to mine integrity that is in me.

Oh let the wickedness of the wicked come to an end; but establish the just: for the righteous God trieth the hearts and reins.

My defence is of God, which saveth the upright in heart.

#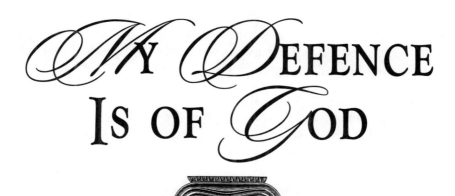

he psalmist declares, *"My defence is of God."* He will not defend himself. He will not ask others to defend him. He rested his case in God's hands. He left it entirely with the Lord.

This seventh Psalm was written during David's flight from Saul's wrath. We find the background for this psalm in II Samuel 24-26. Saul had enlisted three thousand chosen soldiers to find David and to put him to death.

> *He rested his case in God's hands. He left it entirely with the Lord.*

David declared that he had done no wrong to King Saul. Someone had lied to the king. Perhaps someone near the king had told him that David was a threat to his life or to his throne. The truth of the matter is that David never lifted one finger to become king of Israel, even though he was anointed by the prophet Samuel to be king over all Israel. This is "The Psalm to the Slandered Saint."

We have all done wrong and we are not guiltless, but how many of us have been falsely accused or blamed for something for which we were not guilty? How many of us have thought that our name could never be cleared, no matter how hard we tried to explain? Have you ever had anything like this happen in your life?

That is what was going on in David's life. This is why he came to the place of declaring, *"My defence is of God."* It is that simple. At sometime in every person's life, we will deal in some measure with what David dealt with in this psalm.

RESTING IN THE LORD

In verse one David writes under the inspiration of the Spirit of God, *"O LORD my God..."* Notice carefully how that title is given to us in all capital letters. *"O LORD my God..."* When we see the word *"LORD"* spelled in all capital letters in our authorized version of the Bible, it means Jehovah God, the God of the Hebrews, the covenant God of Israel, the Creator God, the God who is the only true and living God.

There is no painless way to follow Jesus Christ.

David said, "Jehovah, You are my God. I trust in no one else." Then he said, *"Save me from all them that persecute me, and deliver me."* Notice the order here. David says, "I am trusting in the You. Lord, deliver me and save me from all of them that persecute me."

Many times we have difficulty with certain people. We say that someone does not like us and that person would like to get us or that someone has said something about us that he or she should not have said. It is impossible to live and not have problems with people.

There is no painless way to follow Jesus Christ. It is impossible to be involved in life and not be misunderstood at times. The real problem that we have is not in our relationships with people. The real problem we have is our unwillingness to trust God. Once we truly put our faith in the Lord and leave our defense in His hands, we can rest in our minds and hearts, no matter what others might do or say. The real struggle, though it may appear to be a "people struggle," is the struggle that we have with trusting the Lord.

I am thankful that I am a Christian. When I say I am Christian, I mean that I have asked God to forgive my sin and I have trusted Christ and Christ alone as my personal Savior. It means my entire hope of heaven is based entirely on Jesus Christ and nothing that I have done or could do. Everything is in Christ, and Christ is everything. He bled and died for my soul's salvation. He paid my sin debt on the cross. When He paid my sin debt, He not only paid for my sin, He tasted death for every man. I can go anywhere in the world and tell people, "Jesus Christ died for you."

Someone explained to me that Christ died for me and that He was buried and rose from the dead. I asked Him to forgive my sin and by faith trusted Him as my Savior. It is easy for me to say that I have trusted Christ as my Savior. It is not so easy to say that I trust Him each day to have victory in my Christian life.

The real problem that we have is not in our relationships with people. The real problem we have is our unwillingness to trust God.

David did not declare, "I am going to match weapons of war with these three thousand men that Saul has chosen." He did not say, "I am going to match weapons of war with King Saul." He did not say, "I am going to try to straighten out what someone has falsely accused me of." He said, *"My defence is of God."* He put the matter in God's hands. There is a *"rest"* in trusting in the Lord that cannot be found anywhere else on earth.

> *There is a "rest" in trusting in the Lord that cannot be found anywhere else on earth.*

As I struggle in my own life or with things that I must deal with in the Lord's work, the real battle is not whether or not I am going to be able to raise enough money for one project or another, or deal with someone who may have some misunderstanding. The real problem is that I am not willing to come in simple child-like faith and rest my case in the hands of God and find the peace that only God can give.

You may be going through something in your home with a child or with your mate, or something on your job may seem so overwhelming that you do not know if you will live through it. But the real struggle is not that struggle; the real struggle is whether you will give that to God and let God see you through it. Come to the place of just giving it to God. You may say, "I don't have much faith." Exercise what faith you have.

There is a wonderful verse of scripture found in Exodus14:14. The Bible says, *"The LORD shall fight for you, and ye shall hold your peace."* These two things go hand in hand. If you have faith to believe that God will fight for you, you will hold your peace. The fact that we do not hold our peace but try to justify ourselves is evidence that we are not trusting God to fight for us.

We tell on ourselves by trying to defend ourselves and talk about what we would do, should do, could do, or what has been done to us. We are broadcasting that we are not trusting God by so much of what we say. The Bible says, *"The LORD shall fight for you, and ye shall hold your peace."* The rest that we find is in trusting the Lord and resting in Him. All of us need this so desperately.

The Bible says in Isaiah 26:3, *"Thou wilt keep him in perfect peace, whose mind is stayed on thee: because he trusteth in thee."* The mind is the real battleground; is it not? We are told in the book of Hebrews that we grow weary in our mind and faint unless we look unto the Lord Jesus.

Paul wrote the church in Corinth and said, *"...bringing into captivity every thought to the obedience of Christ"* (II Corinthians 10:5). This is where the real struggle takes place. You may get an idea or some thought in your mind, something that distracts you from trusting the Lord, something that pulls you away from the direction in which you ought to be going. You must bring that thought into obedience to Christ.

The Bible says in Isaiah 26:3-4, *"Thou wilt keep him in perfect peace, whose mind is stayed on thee: because he trusteth in thee. Trust ye in the LORD for ever: for in the LORD JEHOVAH is everlasting strength."* Remember in our psalm that David was being hunted like an animal. Someone had lied about him and slandered him, but he said, *"My defence is of God."* He was trusting in the Lord.

As we think of resting in the Lord, verse two says, *"Lest he tear my soul like a lion, rending it in pieces, while there is none to deliver."* The lion has quite a time with his prey. He leaves nothing. David knew full well the behavior of a lion. David said, "Lord, what they really want is to be finished with me, to rip me literally to pieces. Deliver me."

> *The fact that we do not hold our peace but try to justify ourselves is evidence that we are not trusting God to fight for us.*

Verses three and four declare, *"O LORD my God, if I have done this; if there be iniquity in my hands; if I have rewarded evil unto him that was at peace with me; (yea, I have delivered him that without cause is mine enemy)."* David is thinking of two occasions. One was at Engedi, when he and his men were in the cave and Saul came into the cave. He could have killed Saul but did not. The other occasion was when David walked down into the plains as Saul was sleeping with three thousand of his men, and God caused a deep sleep to come upon Saul. David's nephew said, "Let me take a spear and run him through. It would only take me one time. I will run the thing through his body all at once and nail him to the earth." David said, "No."

David writes in verse five, *"Let the enemy persecute my soul, and take it; yea, let him tread down my life upon the earth, and lay mine honour in the dust. Selah."* This particular verse makes reference to treading down life upon the earth, a tactic employed in military exploits where people would be drawn by horses and then trampled into the earth underneath the horses hoofs.

David was saying, "If I have done what I am accused of doing, Lord, let me be trampled into the earth." I wish I could speak with that kind of confidence. I wish I could say when spoken against, "Lord if I have opened my mouth, if I have caused harm to someone, let me be trampled into the earth." David said that.

David entered into a peace and a rest that is so seldom found in our lives. He found refuge and a deep hiding place in the Person of Jesus Christ. He found a secure resting place in the Lord that so few of God's children ever know anything about. It comes in "faithing" the Lord. Most often we look at how great our problems are and how weak we are instead of how great our God is.

Verses six and seven say:

> *Arise, O Lord, in thine anger, lift up thyself because of the rage of mine enemies: and awake for me to the judgment that thou hast commanded. So shall the congregation of the people compass thee about: for their sakes therefore return thou on high.*

We have a picture in verse seven of people surrounding Christ, clinging to Him. The rest that we find is in faith. Are you honest enough to say that you are tossed and troubled? Do you have a hard time finding peace of heart? I am going to confess my sin. I let things bother me beyond what I should. I excuse the fact that I am bothered by saying, "I am a compassionate person. I just care. I am a sensitive person." But you see, if you will allow yourself, and if I will allow myself, we will rationalize our faith completely away.

The Lord wants us to come to the place where we are willing to trust Him. What must He put upon us to get us to come to the place where we are willing to trust Him? Do you know why people give their burdens to God? Because the burdens become too great for them to bear.

What if Saul had thirty men instead of three thousand? Perhaps David would have tried to hold them off. As long as we have just got a "little" problem, we will deal with it. If a "little" something is going wrong, we say, "I'll deal with it." As long as it is just a tiny thing in our eyes compared to what it could be, we will attempt to deal with it. But when it becomes so great that it is overwhelming and we know that we cannot handle it, and the only One who can is God, then He crushes us beneath that load until we get to the place where we say, "Dear God, I don't think I am going to make it. All I can do is trust in the Lord."

> *What must He put upon us to get us to come to the place where we are willing to trust Him? Do you know why people give their burdens to God? Because the burdens become too great for them to bear.*

This is how God deals with His children. The Lord smiles because we find the rest in Him which He wanted us to find in the beginning, but we would not trust Him. How

great must the burden become before we cast it on Him? Rest in the Lord. *"My defence is of God."*

REAPING WHAT WE SOW

We are all going to reap because we all sow In Galatians 6:7-9 the Bible says,

> *Be not deceived; God is not mocked: for whatsoever a man soweth, that shall he also reap. For he that soweth to his flesh shall of the flesh reap corruption; but he that soweth to the Spirit shall of the Spirit reap life everlasting. And let us not be weary in well doing: for in due season we shall reap, if we faint not.*

To really believe that people are going to reap what they have sown is an expression of faith in God. Not only do we all sow, we all also reap. We not only reap what we sow, we reap more than we sow.

If a farmer sows corn, he reaps corn; if he sows green beans, he reaps green beans. Whatever we sow, we are going to reap. Every day I plant things in life that I am going to reap in some tomorrow. It is going to be more than I have sown. I can sow to the flesh, or I can sow to the Spirit.

Look again at Psalm seven. The Bible says in verse eight, *"The LORD shall judge the people: judge me, O LORD, according to my righteousness, and according to mine integrity that is in me."* I love the word *"righteousness,"* and I love the word *"integrity."* We are not righteous in ourselves. If we are righteous and live righteously, it is because we have the imputed righteousness of Jesus Christ on our account. There is nothing good in us. The Bible says in Isaiah 64:6 that all of our righteousnesses, all of our good works, are as filthy rags. The best we can do is not good enough to get us to heaven.

I remember when I trusted Jesus Christ as my Savior. Because I trusted Him as my Savior and received the grace of God into my life, God started to deal with me about living for Him. As I started living for the Lord, there were things that I did not want to do any longer because they were not honoring to Christ. At that time, I was the only member of my family that was a Christian. When I was with my family, there were things that we did together as a family that I no longer felt comfortable doing because I was a Christian. I knew the Lord did not want me to do those things. From my perspective, I was doing for Christ what I believed Christ wanted me to do. I was separating myself from activities I thought were dishonoring to the Lord and trying to honor the Lord in my behavior.

At one time, as a family we would go to the theater. I felt I could not live a strong, Christian life going to the movies. In my family, people did not think there was anything wrong with social drinking. When I became a Christian, I did not think Christians ought to use alcohol as a beverage because the Bible speaks against it.

My family loved me and they still love me, but some may have said, "Oh, he thinks he is too good for us now." That was never the case. Some of you who have tried to live for Christ have experienced the same thing. At times, we have been overly zealous, and we have said things as Christians to unsaved family members we should not have said. We just wanted them saved; we wanted them to know the joy we had found in Christ.

God deals with His children about what they are sowing because He knows they are going to reap what they sow.

The fact is, we all sow and we all reap, and God deals with His children about what they are sowing because He knows they are going to reap what they sow. David said, *"Judge me."* He talked about his integrity. No one can take integrity from you. To lose

93

it you must give it up. Integrity is walking before God in honesty, fearing the Lord, living an upright life and being trustworthy.

No one can take integrity from you. To lose it you must give it up. Integrity is walking before God in honesty, fearing the Lord, living an upright life and being trustworthy.

David says in verse nine, *"Oh let the wickedness of the wicked come to an end; but establish the just."* In other words, what the wicked are doing will finally come to an end, but the just will be established. The wicked are going one way; the just are going the other. *"For the righteous God trieth the hearts and reins."*

Many people think they can live any way they please without consequences. You cannot live any way you please and get by with it. You may say, "If I am not a Christian, I can get by with it." Yes, you can, but you are going to die and go to hell. If you are a Christian, you cannot live any way you please and get by with it. When you die you are going to heaven, and it must be dealt with here and now.

The Bible says in verses ten and eleven, *"My defence is of God, which saveth the upright in heart. God judgeth the righteous, and God is angry with the wicked every day."* This is a fearful expression. God is angry with the wicked every day. How would you like to have God angry with you everyday? If you are not one of God's children, you have identified yourself with a group that God is angry with everyday.

Verse twelve says, *"If he turn not, he will whet his sword; he hath bent his bow, and made it ready."* He is sharpening the sword for judgement. The bow is ready for judgement. We read in verse thirteen, *"He hath also prepared for him the instruments of death; he ordaineth his arrows against the persecutors."* Notice what He says about the wicked in verse fourteen, *"Behold, he*

94

travaileth with iniquity, and hath conceived mischief, and brought forth falsehood."

When we talk about travail and conception, which comes first—travail or conception? We know the answer is conception. Has the Bible got the order mixed up here? Of course not! Think and pray concerning this matter.

There is conception, then there is travail in the birthing of a child. But the Bible says that the wicked travail, then they conceive. What does this mean? It means that a person without God is always tossed to and fro, like angry waves of the sea, always torn, always travailing. He is always moving, churning in life. Then some evil idea is conceived. When he gives birth to the idea, what is it? It brings forth falsehood. It is a lie.

David said, "I understand the wicked. They are always travailing, then they conceive an idea and they bring forth falsehood. This is their wicked work." He said in verse fifteen that the wicked *"made a pit, and digged it, and is fallen into the ditch which he made."* He reaped what he sowed.

I tremble for some people who say things they should not say. I tremble with what the wicked are going to have to deal with at the hands of our holy God. Dear child of God, be careful with your words. Be careful with your deeds. We reap what we sow. The wicked dig a ditch. They seek to harm others, and instead of harming others, the harm they seek for others comes to them. They reap what they sow.

The Bible says in verse sixteen, *"His mischief shall return upon his own head, and his violent dealing shall come down upon his own pate."* The word *"pate"* means the crown of the head, the top of the head. It hits him in the crown of the head. Are we resting in the Lord? *"My defence is of God."* Commit your way to the Lord. Remember, we will reap what we sow.

REJOICING IN THE LORD

David is still being sought after, and in the midst of it he rejoices, saying in verse seventeen, *"I will praise the Lord according to his righteousness: and will sing praise to the name of the Lord most high."* Why? Not because of what the Lord has done, but because of who God is. David said, "Because of who God is, I know what He is going to do." Is this not a blessing? In other words, he prayed the Lord would take action.

In verse six, David asked God to rise and take action. The Lord had not yet risen. *"I will praise the Lord according to his righteousness."* David was declaring, "Before He acts, I know how He is going to act, and when He does, because of who He is, I am going to praise Him for it." David chose to *"sing praise to the name of the Lord most high."*

In the seventeenth verse of the seventh Psalm, the psalmist actually says, "I am shouting and rejoicing in the Lord, though God has not yet acted on my behalf. I am shouting because of who God is, and I know what He is going to do." That is living by faith.

In New York City, there is a man and his family who are serving God and winning souls. They are not Baptists, but they love the Lord. The pastor started out as a business man. His father-in-law asked him to take a church as a layman. God spoke to his heart while he was filling in only as a lay person. As a matter of fact, he was filling in for two churches, and then he recognized that God wanted him in the ministry, and he surrendered his life to preach.

The man took a little handful of believers in a difficult place in New York City, and now the church has grown to a church of thousands. Early in that ministry, they came home one day and their sixteen-year-old daughter was gone. She had run away. She had been devoured by that city. The mother and the father began to weep.

They could not find their daughter. Two years passed. People in the church realized what a burden these parents were under because their daughter was away from God and in sin. They said to the pastor, "Pastor, we just need to stop everything in this church and fast and pray that God brings her home." And they did. While the daughter was away, the mother wrote these words,

> In my moments of fear, through every pain, every
>   tear, there is a God who has been faithful to me,
> When my strength was all gone, when my heart had
>   no song, still in love, He proved faithful to me.
> Every word He has promised is true.
> What I thought was impossible, I have seen my
>   God do.
> He has been faithful to me.
> Looking back, His love and mercy I see.
> Though in my heart I have questioned, even failed
>   to believe,
> He has been faithful, faithful to me.

Then another verse:

> When my heart looked away, the many times I could
>   not pray, still my God He was faithful to me.
> The days I spent so selfishly, reaching out for what
>   pleased me, even then God was faithful to me.
> Every time I come back to Him, He is waiting with
>   open arms.
> I see once again, He has been faithful, faithful to me.
> Looking back his love and mercy I see.
> Though in my heart I have questioned, even failed
>   to believe.
> Yet, He has been faithful, faithful to me.

They prayed for that girl. Soon after that time of special prayer, she came home and said, "Somebody is praying for me. God has dealt with my heart. I am coming home to the Lord. I am brokenhearted over my sin."

Today, she is married to a minister, serving the Lord Jesus and living for God. God gave her mother a song in her time of grief; she believed the Lord was going to do what the Lord alone could do. If we are going to live the Christian life the Bible speaks of, it is a life that learns to praise God for who He is, knowing that He is going to do right even though the answer has not yet come.

David said, *"My defence is of God."*

PSALM 8

O Lord our Lord, how excellent is thy name in all the earth! who hast set thy glory above the heavens.

Out of the mouth of babes and sucklings hast thou ordained strength because of thine enemies, that thou mightest still the enemy and the avenger.

When I consider thy heavens, the work of thy fingers, the moon and the stars, which thou hast ordained;

What is man, that thou art mindful of him? and the son of man, that thou visitest him?

For thou hast made him a little lower than the angels, and hast crowned him with glory and honour.

Thou madest him to have dominion over the works of thy hands; thou hast put all things under his feet:

All sheep and oxen, yea, and the beasts of the field;

The fowl of the air, and the fish of the sea, and whatsoever passeth through the paths of the seas.

O Lord our Lord, how excellent is thy name in all the earth!

CHAPTER
EIGHT

WHAT IS MAN?

 salm eight is a beautiful psalm that begins and ends with the wonder and exaltation of God. It is a psalm about God, God's creation, Christ, and man. Like all else in life, this psalm begins and ends with God. Are you prepared to meet Him?

The Bible says in Psalm 8:1-9,

> *O LORD our Lord, how excellent is thy name in all the earth! who hast set thy glory above the heavens. Out of the mouth of babes and sucklings hast thou ordained strength because of thine enemies, that thou mightest still the enemy and the avenger. When I consider thy heavens, the work of thy fingers, the moon and the stars, which thou hast ordained; what is man, that thou art mindful of him? and the son of man, that thou visitest him? For thou hast made him a little lower than the angels, and hast crowned him with glory and honour. Thou madest him to have*

dominion over the works of thy hands; thou hast put all things under his feet: all sheep and oxen, yea, and the beasts of the field; the fowl of the air, and the fish of the sea, and whatsoever passeth through the paths of the sea. O Lord our Lord, how excellent is thy name in all the earth!

Notice the piercing question in the heart of this psalm, *"What is man that thou art mindful of him?"* What is man?

The Bible says in the first verse of Psalm eight, *"O Lord our Lord."* I hope you can sincerely use the personal pronoun "our." *"O Lord our Lord, how excellent is thy name in all the earth!"* The last verse says, *"O Lord our Lord, how excellent is thy name in all the earth!"*

What is man? When the Bible asks a question, it provides an answer for that question. The Bible declares in Isaiah 40:6,

The voice said, Cry. And he said, What shall I cry? All flesh is grass, and all the goodliness thereof is as the flower of the field: the grass withereth, the flower fadeth; because the spirit of the Lord bloweth upon it: surely the people is grass. The grass withereth, the flower fadeth: but the word of our God shall stand for ever.

Consider man as he comes and goes, as a vapor that appears for a little while and soon vanishes away. He seems so insignificant, but man is the crown of God's creation.

As the psalmist stepped out to see the starry heaven at night, he thought of all God's creation. When he thought of all the glory and grandeur of God's handiwork, he thought of his own insignificance. God gave him these words to pen, *"What is man?"* In other words, "In light of all God's creation, what is man that God is mindful of him?"

102

In the light of all that God is and has done, what is man that God is mindful of him? Psalm eight answers this question.

I am deeply concerned about the home and the family, but we are not going to be able to help the home until we understand the answer to this question—*"What is man?"* This question refers to all mankind, both men and women.

Many people have the idea that a mate is going to bring complete fulfillment to them and that they are going to live happily ever after. But there is no peace, no purpose, no fulfillment in life until we understand and answer this question—*"What is man?"*

Once we have answered this question from God's Word, we will realize that the only real peace and purpose comes through our individual relationship and fellowship with God and not from another human being. There has never been a woman, no matter how wonderful she is, who can bring total satisfaction to a man. There has never been a man, no matter how great he is, who can bring complete satisfaction, fulfillment, and purpose to a woman. There have never been children, as compliant and as beautiful as some may be, who can bring purpose, meaning, and fulfillment to others in life. God has designed life so that there is no way to be all He wants us to be apart from Him. We are spiritual beings, and this places an absolute necessity on knowing God.

Once we have answered this question from God's Word, we will realize that the only real peace and purpose comes through our individual relationship and fellowship with God and not from another human being.

As we think about our own behavior, we realize how good we are at blaming others for our unhappiness and our lack of purpose and fulfillment. "This woman is not providing for me what I need," or "This man is not providing for me what I need," or "These children are driving me crazy." The truth of the matter is, God has designed life so that we cannot find what we truly need in people; it must be found in Him.

> *Like all else in life, this psalm begins and ends with God.*

The Bible says in the second verse of Psalm eight, *"Out of the mouth of babes and sucklings hast thou ordained strength because of thine enemies, that thou mightest still the enemy and the avenger."* The Lord Jesus Christ makes reference to this verse in the New Testament. Psalm eight continues in verse three, *"When I consider thy heavens, the work of thy fingers, the moon, and the stars, which thou hast ordained."*

Here the psalmist draws a night picture, a picture of darkness, speaking of the moon and stars. We learn more about God in times of darkness than we do in times of light. We learn more about God in hours of great need than we do in hours of great victory. We learn more of God in the dark valleys than we do on the bright mountaintops.

Psalm 8:3-5 says,

> *When I consider thy heavens, the work of thy fingers, the moon and the stars, which thou hast ordained; what is man, that thou art mindful of him? and the son of man, that thou visitest him? For thou hast made him a little lower than the angels, and hast crowned him with glory and honour.*

Notice the word *"little."* This is not referring to stature or size, but rather to time; it means "for a little while." The verse refers to the Lord Jesus Christ who became a man without ceasing to be God. For

a little while He was made lower than the angels to suffer and bleed and die for us. We know this is true because the New Testament gives a commentary on this verse. We will return to this a little later in this chapter.

The Bible says in verse six, *"Thou madest him to have dominion."* Notice the word *"dominion."* This was God's intent and purpose for man. *"Thou madest him to have dominion over the works of thy hands; thou has put all things under his feet."*

> *As we think about our own behavior, we realize how good we are at blaming others for our unhappiness and our lack of purpose and fulfillment.*

At this time, man can in no way have absolute dominion over anything because he has refused to allow God to have dominion over him. When God created man, He gave a name to man, but he allowed man to name everything else in creation. He had dominion.

The Word of God says in verses six through eight,

> *Thou madest him to have dominion over the works of thy hands; thou hast put all things under his feet: all sheep and oxen, yea, and the beasts of the field; the fowl of the air, and the fish of the sea, and whatsoever passeth through the paths of the seas.*

Again, we start and we stop with the excellency, the glory, the wonder, and the grandeur of God. Verse nine declares, *"O LORD our Lord, how excellent is thy name in all the earth!"*

MAN IN COMPASSION

What is man? Let us consider man in compassion. This is not the compassion of man, but the compassion of God for man. Jeremiah 31:3 says, *"I have loved thee with an everlasting love."* He cares for me. The amazing thing about this question is not the first part, *"What is man?"* The amazing thing is the second part, *"That thou art mindful of him."* The amazing thing is that God remembers us and that God cares for us. God has compassion on us. We are not insignificant; we are most significant to God.

> *We learn more about God in times of darkness than we do in times of light.*

"What is man that thou art mindful of him?" It is as though the psalmist stood in awe and said, "Lord, the thing that is incomprehensible to me is that You love me as You do."

Meditate on Job 7:17, *"What is man, that thou shouldest magnify him? and that thou shouldest set thine heart upon him?"* God sets His heart upon man.

What is man? In our world, we have lost the emphasis God places on the individual. People give their attention more to animals and plants than human beings. This is not the emphasis God has. God has made mankind not just for time, but for eternity.

The unbelieving world says, "Save the whales and kill the babies." The world says, "Spare the monkeys pain and afflict pain on the unborn." When God sees this world, He places the emphasis on mankind. He has compassion on people.

Of course, God cares for all His creation, and all of us should be responsible in our citizenship. In one sense, we are citizens of our planet. I understand this, and I do not mean to belittle this, but let us

never emphasize it as others emphasize it to the neglect of what God emphasizes. *"What is man that thou art mindful of him?"*

There is a lady in our church who is not just a lady to me–she is my wife. I place emphasis on her; she is my wife. She is different from all the others. She has my compassion. She has my special care. I look after her.

At this time, man can in no way have absolute dominion over anything because he has refused to allow God to have dominion over him.

The psalmist said, "In all of creation, when I consider how great and grand the stars and planets, the seas, the animals of the earth–when I see it all, I think, *'What is man that thou art mindful of him?'"*

The church in which I serve is not just any church. It is the church God has allowed me to pastor. He has placed me there as a shepherd. The people have my devotion, my love, my concern, my prayers, and by God's grace, I hope they have my leadership.

Man is bathed in compassion. Our God cares. *"What is man that thou art mindful of him?"* I am overwhelmed with the thought that God has placed such attention, such direction, and such compassion on me.

MAN IN CREATION

God's Word tells us in Genesis 1:26, *"And God said, Let us make man in our image."* Man did not evolve from some lower primate. He did not begin as a one-cell amoeba or come from some sort of gas explosion. Man was created a full-grown, perfect being and placed in a dispensation of innocence by the very hand of God. This is how he began.

We have already noticed the word *"dominion"* in Psalm eight. We see it also in Genesis 1:26-27. The Bible says,

> *And God said, Let us make man in our image, after our likeness: and let them have dominion over the fish of the sea, and over the fowl of the air, and over the cattle, and over all the earth, and over every creeping thing that creepeth upon the earth. So God created man in his own image, in the image of God created he him; male and female created he them.*

Notice what God says about man's intelligence. Genesis 2:19 says,

> *And out of the ground the LORD God formed every beast of the field, and every fowl of the air; and brought them unto Adam to see what he would call them: and whatsoever Adam called every living creature, that was the name thereof.*

God created man and named him. Then He brought everything He had created before Adam and said, "You name each thing I have created." Verse twenty says, *"And Adam gave names to all cattle, and to the fowl of the air, and to every beast of the field; but for Adam there was not found an help meet for him."*

Man was created in the image of God. What does it mean for God to declare, *"Let us make man in our own image,"* and *"...in the image of God made He him; male and female"?* God created man with a spirit, soul, and body.

In our spirit is our God-consciousness; in our spirit we relate to God. In our soul we possess intellect, emotion, and will. Our bodies enable us to relate to the world around us through the five senses God has given us. In our spirit, God speaks to us, and our spirit works

with our soul in intellect, emotion, and will. Through our bodies, we relate to the world around us.

When people are dead spiritually, the only thing they can relate to is the world. They cannot relate to God. This is why the Lord Jesus Christ said we *"must be born again."* Without the new birth, we are dead in our trespasses and sins. A man is spiritually blind if he is without Jesus Christ, but he is also a dead man. The Bible says in Ephesians 2:1, *"And you hath he quickened, who were dead in trespasses and sins."*

> *We have lost the emphasis God places on the individual.*

If you have never trusted Jesus Christ as your personal Savior, you are dead in your trespasses and sins. You are lost without God, without hope, and without a Redeemer. You can respond to God as He deals with you by His Holy Spirit. You can do all you want to do to be a better person, a better husband, a better wife, but it is impossible for you to be all God meant for you to be when you are dead spiritually. He created us spirit, soul, and body.

The Bible says in I Corinthians 2:10-14,

> *But God hath revealed them unto us by his Spirit: for the Spirit searcheth all things, yea, the deep things of God. For what man knoweth the things of a man, save the spirit of man which is in him? even so the things of God knoweth no man, but the Spirit of God. Now we have received, not the spirit of the world, but the spirit which is of God; that we might know the things that are freely given to us of God. Which things also we speak, not in the words which man's wisdom teacheth, but which the Holy Ghost teacheth; comparing spiritual things with spiritual. But the natural man receiveth not the things of the Spirit of*

God: for they are foolishness unto him: neither can he know them, because they are spiritually discerned.

Remember, we are created spirit, soul, and body. I Thessalonians 5:23 says, *"And the very God of peace sanctify you wholly; and I pray God your whole spirit and soul and body be preserved blameless unto the coming of our Lord Jesus Christ."*

> *Do not expect another human being to do for you what only God can do for you.*

A man may say that he wants to be a happy man, that he wants to be the right kind of man who has peace and fulfillment in life. He says he is going to go out and find a wife, and he thinks he will be happy because he finds the right kind of wife. No, he will not be happy simply because he found the right wife.

A woman says she is going to meet and marry Mr. Right and they will be happy, but there is something still not right. They think that having children will make them happy and that everything will be just like it should be. They are blessed with the birth of a child and they are excited about it, but before long they find out that even that child does not bring the fulfillment, peace, and purpose so desperately needed. What is missing? People cannot bring peace, purpose, satisfaction, or fulfillment to our lives. Only God can.

I never shall forget a man saying to me about a particular woman, "She just cannot meet all my needs." Someone needed to tell him that no woman could meet all his needs, so I told him. Only God can meet that spiritual need, and as He meets that spiritual need, that man can relate to others who love the Lord and follow the Lord.

If there is oneness in a marriage, there must be oneness in spirit, soul, and body. There is oneness in spirit when we both walk with

God and know the Lord and listen as He speaks to us. We love Him and love His Word. The same Holy Spirit gives us direction.

There is oneness in soul as we agree intellectually, emotionally, and of our own will share the same goals and desires for life. Then there is oneness in body. In God's Word, the order is spirit, soul, then body.

What is man? God has created man in His own image. There is unity in spirit, soul, and body. God has designed man so that he can find peace in his relationship with God and bring that peace into his marriage relationship, into his home, and into his family. Do not expect another human being to do for you what only God can do for you.

MAN IN CHRIST

What is man in Christ? In Psalm eight, we see that we are lost. We are fallen creatures. We are no longer people who have dominion over the beasts of the field, the fowl of the air, and the animals in the sea. The first Adam has fallen; he sinned against God. Everything we had was lost in that Adamic head of the human race. We are lost. We are plunging toward hell, ruined by the fall.

There must be a second Adam, a perfect One to come. How can He redeem us? He must be made, for a little while, lower than the angels. He who is above the angels, whose name is above every name, must for a while become lower than the angels in order to bear the sin of the whole world in His body, to pay our sin debt, to bleed and die so that man can be what God meant for him to be.

He became a man—not an angel, but a sinless man— without ceasing to be God.

The Bible says in Psalm 8:4-5, *"What is man, that thou art mindful of him? and the son of man, that thou visitest him? For thou hast*

made him a little lower than the angels, and hast crowned him with glory and honour."

This psalm is not just about man; it is about what Christ came to do for man. We are thinking not only about what man is in compassion, what man is in creation, but also what man is in Christ. Are you in Christ?

In Matthew chapter twenty-one, the Lord Jesus was on His way to bleed and die for us. The Bible says in Matthew 21:12-14,

> *And Jesus went into the temple of God, and cast out all them that sold and bought in the temple, and overthrew the tables of the moneychangers, and the seats of them that sold doves, and said unto them, It is written, My house shall be called the house of prayer; but ye have made it a den of thieves. And the blind and the lame came to him in the temple; and he healed them.*

This is a beautiful scene. The Bible says, *"And the blind and the lame came to him in the temple; and he healed them."* Think of the heartache in the lives of those people, the years of anxiety, pitiful pain, and accusations concerning their illnesses which were mistakenly associated with sin. Think of their deliverance and how wonderful it was when Jesus Christ touched their blinded eyes and for the first time ever they could see. How wonderful it was when He touched their lame limbs and they could leap and walk with joy. It must have been an exciting time.

The Bible says in verse fifteen, *"And when the chief priests and scribes saw the wonderful things that he did..."* These wonderful things were the miracles they saw the Lord perform on the blind and the lame. They saw these things *"and the children crying in the temple, and saying, Hosanna to the son of David,"* and *"they were sore displeased."*

The children were excited. Perhaps many of the children were related to these blind and lame people. The chief priests and scribes wanted it all stopped. They were *"sore displeased."* The Bible says in verse sixteen, *"And said unto him, hearest thou what these say? And Jesus saith unto them, Yea; have ye never read, Out of the mouths of babes and sucklings thou hast perfected praise?"*

Christ was quoting from the eighth Psalm. We know that Psalm eight speaks of Christ being praised for what He came to do for fallen man because Jesus Christ quotes from it and identifies Himself with it.

In I Corinthians chapter fifteen, the apostle Paul writes under the inspiration of the Spirit of God concerning Psalm eight. The Bible says in I Corinthians 15:20-22,

But now is Christ risen from the dead, and become the firstfruits of them that slept. For since by man came death, by man came also the resurrection of the dead. For as in Adam all die, even so in Christ shall all be made alive.

When sin came by the fall, we lost this fellowship with God. We became children of the Devil by nature. We had no home to look forward to but hell and no life on earth but bondage.

In other words, God wants to make man what He meant for man to be and return to him even more than what he lost in the fall. In I Corinthians 15:23-28 the Bible says,

But every man in his own order: Christ the firstfruits; afterward they that are Christ's at his coming. Then cometh the end, when he shall have delivered up the kingdom to God, even the Father; when he shall have put down all rule and all authority and power. For

> *he must reign, till he hath put all enemies under his feet. The last enemy that shall be destroyed is death. For he hath put all things under his feet. But when he saith all things are put under him, it is manifest that he is excepted, which did put all things under him. And when all things shall be subdued unto him, then shall the Son also himself be subject unto him that put all things under him, that God may be all in all.*

Notice the statement *"all things under his feet."* What does this mean? He was quoting from Psalm eight. He said that God gave man dominion, but he lost that dominion. Jesus Christ is going to have dominion over everything. Why did He come? He came to present that dominion to man and to enable man to rule with Him. What we gain through the cross is more than we ever possessed in the garden.

Part of Hebrews chapter two forms a commentary on the eighth Psalm. The Bible says in Hebrews 2:5-6,

> *For unto the angels hath he not put in subjection the world to come, whereof we speak. But one in a certain place testified, saying, What is man, that thou art mindful of him? or the son of man, that thou visitest him?*

He quotes from Psalm eight, and then he explains the psalm. The Bible says in Hebrews 2:7-8,

> *Thou madest him a little lower than the angels; thou crownedst him with glory and honour, and didst set him over the works of thy hands: thou hast put all things in subjection under his feet. For in that he put all in subjection under him, he left nothing that is not put under him.*

It is not yet placed under Him, but it is going to be. Who is He talking about? What is He talking about? Verse nine says, *"But we see Jesus, who was made a little lower than the angels for the suffering of death."*

He was made lower than the angels so that He could suffer and bleed and die for us. Why did He suffer and bleed and die for us? God saw what man is without Christ: going to hell forever, incomplete, lost, dead, blind, and under the wrath of God. This is not what He created us to be, so He sent Christ from heaven and made Him a little lower than the angels. Why was He made lower than the angels? The Bible answers this in verse nine, *"For the suffering of death, crowned with glory and honour; that he by the grace of God should taste death for every man."*

We read on in Hebrews 2:10-18,

> *For it became him, for whom are all things, and by whom are all things, in bringing many sons unto glory, to make the captain of their salvation perfect through sufferings. For both he that sanctifieth and they who are sanctified are all of one: for which cause he is not ashamed to call them brethren, saying, I will declare thy name unto my brethren, in the midst of the church will I sing praise unto thee. And again, I will put my trust in him. And again, Behold I and the children which God hath given me. Forasmuch then as the children are partakers of flesh and blood, he also himself likewise took part of the same; that through death he might destroy him that had the power of death, that is, the devil; and deliver them, who through fear of death were all their lifetime subject to bondage. For verily he took not on him the nature of angels; but he took on him the seed of Abraham. Wherefore in all things it behoved him to be made like unto his brethren, that he might be a merciful*

and faithful high priest in things pertaining to God,
to make reconciliation for the sins of the people. For
in that he himself hath suffered being tempted, he is
able to succour them that are tempted.

This passage says that the Lord Jesus Christ willingly came to earth. He became a man–not an angel, but a sinless man–without ceasing to be God. Why did He become a man? He became a man because in the garden God created man in His own image to walk with Him, to fellowship with Him, and to know Him. He created man with a spirit, soul, and body to have dominion over the fowl of the air, the beasts of the field, and the fish of the sea.

When sin came by the fall, we lost this fellowship with God. We became children of the Devil by nature. We had no home to look forward to but hell and no life on earth but bondage. God sent His own dear Son to defeat the devil, to taste death for every man, to suffer our penalty for sin, to be buried in a borrowed tomb, and to come forth from the grave alive forevermore.

The Devil could say to God, "Look at man! What a failure and disgrace he is. You made him and he will not even acknowledge You. You made him and he denies that You even exist." But in Christ, God can declare to Satan, "Now look at him. He has been born again. He loves Me. He knows Me. He walks with Me. I speak to him and he speaks with Me. I am going to deliver him someday and give him a perfect body."

When we see Christ, we shall be like Him, *"for we shall see Him as He is"* (I John 3:2). Think of what man can be in Christ, what he is in Christ, and what he shall be someday in Christ. It is glorious!

We cannot make it alone, and we cannot be what God wants us to be through another human being. We must stop thinking that our failure is because of someone else. We must understand that what we need is a personal relationship with God. We blame others too often

for things for which they are not responsible. I am responsible for walking with God and being a better man. The same is true of you.

"What is man that thou art mindful of him?" My heart is overcome with joy thinking that God is mindful of me. I am not alone. I am never alone, and I will never be forsaken. Jesus Christ is my Savior.

Psalm 9:9-17

The LORD also will be a refuge for the oppressed, a refuge in times of trouble.

And they that know thy name will put their trust in thee: for thou, LORD, hast not forsaken them that seek thee.

Sing praises to the LORD, which dwelleth in Zion: declare among the people his doings.

When he maketh inquisition for blood, he remembereth them: he forgetteth not the cry of the humble.

Have mercy upon me, O LORD; consider my trouble which I suffer of them that hate me, thou that liftest me up from the gates of death:

That I may shew forth all thy praise in the gates of the daughter of Zion: I will rejoice in thy salvation.

The heathen are sunk down in the pit that they made: in the net which they hid is their own foot taken.

The LORD is known by the judgment which he executeth: the wicked is snared in the work of his own hands. Higgaion. Selah.

The wicked shall be turned into hell, and all the nations that forget God.

CHAPTER NINE

ALL THE NATIONS THAT FORGET GOD

 ations are made up of people, and people forget God. What place does the Lord have in your heart at this moment?

The ninth Psalm deals with God's complete victory over all His adversaries. The contrast of the righteous and the wicked is dealt with here in Psalm nine and in Psalm ten. When we come to the tenth Psalm, God deals particularly with the wicked in Israel. In Psalm nine, God deals with the wicked outside of Israel. The Bible says in Psalm 9:17 that there are nations that forget God, and all the nations that forget God will be turned into hell.

No one likes to talk about hell. But it must be dealt with as we teach and preach the whole counsel of God. It was our Lord Jesus Christ who said that a man died and went to hell.

> *And in hell he lift up his eyes, being in torments, and seeth Abraham afar off, and Lazarus in his bosom. And he cried and said, Father Abraham, have mercy on me, and send Lazarus, that he may dip the*

*tip of his finger in water, and cool my tongue; for I
am tormented in this flame* (Luke 16:23-24).

This is what the Lord Jesus Christ said. Think of it! He declared
hell to be real! And the Bible says in Psalm 9:17 that *"all the nations
that forget God"* will be turned into hell. When I read this statement,
my heart is stirred for my own nation.

Though it was not a Christian home, I was raised in what could
be called a "God and country" home. It was a home of great respect
for our heritage as a nation. I grew up as a boy "thinking" that I
lived in a Christian America. Even if people did not attend church,
everyone I knew believed in God, the only true and living God. And
they recognized that it was God's good hand that had been upon this
nation. In this present hour, all of us know this has changed. Think
seriously about our nation in this verse, *"The wicked shall be turned
into hell, and all the nations that forget God."* Why do people forget
God? Nations are made up of individuals. Why do individuals forget
God? Why do you and I forget? The Lord gives His people Israel a
warning in Deuteronomy 6:4-12,

*Hear, O Israel: The LORD our God is one LORD:and
thou shalt love the LORD thy God with all thine heart,
and with all thy soul, and with all thy might. And these
words, which I command thee this day, shall be in
thine heart: and thou shalt teach them diligently unto
thy children, and shalt talk of them when thou sittest
in thine house, and when thou walkest by the way, and
when thou liest down, and when thou risest up. And
thou shalt bind them for a sign upon thine hand, and
they shall be as frontlets between thine eyes. And thou
shalt write them upon the posts of thy house, and on
thy gates. And it shall be, when the LORD thy God shall
have brought thee into the land which he sware unto
thy fathers, to Abraham, to Isaac, and to Jacob, to*

give thee great and goodly cities, which thou buildedst not, and houses full of all good things, which thou filledst not, and wells digged, which thou diggedst not, vineyards and olive trees, which thou plantedst not; when thou shalt have eaten and be full; then beware lest thou forget the LORD, which brought thee forth out of the land of Egypt, from the house of bondage.

Our God said, "Forgetting Me is not a problem when you need Me; it is not a problem when you can't make it without Me. But when you get in the land and taste of all the good things that I have blessed you with, then beware lest you forget Me." History reveals to us that no nation was able to deal with prosperity.

It is estimated that eighty million Americans do not have a copy of the Bible. We need to "reseed" our nation with the Word of God.

In the founding of this great nation, there were many evidences that God had a special purpose for this country. On the public buildings in our nation's capital, our forefathers left records of their faith in God. In the White House, the President's residence, we find, among other things, John Adams' prayer: "I pray heaven to bestow the best of blessings on this house and all that shall hereafter inhabit it. May none but honest and wise men ever rule under this roof." On the Supreme Court building we find the Ten Commandments. In the House of Representatives, above the Speaker's chair, an inscription states, "In God we trust." In the Capitol building, portrait after portrait display God's leading in the founding of our nation. National buildings throughout the Capital city testify of faith in God with their many verses and inscriptions. But now we live in a land of people who have forgotten God. We work among those who have forgotten Him. We live among those who have forgotten Him.

On the Lord's Day, ball fields are crowded with people, recreational parks are filled. Sunday is no longer a holy day.

The heart of the matter is that we have forgotten God. Immorality is preceded by idolatry. Why such behavior? Why such fear? Why are children no longer safe in public places? We have forgotten God!

We have lived to witness a time in the history of our nation where we have forgotten God. In Romans 1:19-20 we see the fruit of it, *"Because that which may be known of God is manifest in them; for God hath shewed it unto them. For the invisible things of him from the creation of the world are clearly seen, being understood by the things that are made, even his eternal power and Godhead; so that they are without excuse."* God makes Himself known. In His Word, the Bible, He reveals Himself to us in written words. It is estimated that eighty million Americans do not have a copy of the Bible. We need to "reseed" our nation with the Word of God.

For the invisible things of him from the creation of the world are clearly seen, being understood by the things that are made, even his eternal power and Godhead; so that they are without excuse : because that, when they knew God, they glorified him not as God, neither were thankful; but became vain in their imaginations, and their foolish heart was darkened. Professing themselves to be wise, they became fools (Romans 1:20-22).

We live in a nation of millions who profess themselves to be wise, but have become fools. They know everything and nothing at the same time! We brag about our intelligence, we store things in our computers, cram our minds with information, and reject the truth.

The things we read about that are happening in our land are shocking! At least they should be. The most serious danger we have in this country is not found on a list of evils almost anyone could give. The heart of the matter is that we have forgotten God. Immorality is preceded by idolatry. Why such behavior? Why such fear? Why are children no longer safe in public places? We have forgotten God!

WHOLEHEARTED FAITH
IN GOD IS ESSENTIAL

The psalmist says in Psalm 9:1, *"I will praise thee, O LORD, with my whole heart."* He was saying, "Not halfheartedly, but I will praise thee with my whole heart!" The psalmist David says, *"I will praise thee, O LORD, with my whole heart; I will shew forth all thy marvellous works. I will be glad and rejoice in thee."* This is a decision we must make.

Notice that the psalmist says again and again, *"I will..."* He says,

"I will praise thee, O LORD, with my whole heart."

"I will shew forth all thy marvellous works."

"I will be glad and rejoice in thee."

"I will sing praise to thy name, O thou most High."

Every one of us can start right here. "I will do these four things!" Wholehearted faith requires a commitment of our will to God. Meditate upon these four tremendous *"I wills."*

He continues in verses three and four, *"When mine enemies are turned back, they shall fall and perish at thy presence."* Notice what he says about the Lord, *"For thou hast maintained my right and my cause."* He did not say, "I have..." This is what we think. "Lord, I've

123

kept it on the straight and narrow." I hear people say when they give their testimonies, "I have tried all of my life to do right. I...I...I..."

If we are what we should be, it is because of the grace of God. It is nothing we can brag about ourselves. The psalmist had it right. *"Thou hast maintained my right and my cause; thou satest in the throne judging right."* God is still on the throne. He has never relinquished that. In the worst of times, God is still on the throne. He has never given it up.

GOD IS OUR REFUGE IN TIMES OF TROUBLE

The Bible says in Psalm 9:5-9,

> *Thou hast rebuked the heathen, thou hast destroyed the wicked, thou hast put out their name for ever and ever. O thou enemy, destructions are come to a perpetual end: and thou hast destroyed cities; their memorial is perished with them. But the Lord shall endure for ever: he hath prepared his throne for judgment. And he shall judge the world in righteousness, he shall minister judgment to the people in uprightness. The Lord also will be a refuge for the oppressed, a refuge in times of trouble.*

When you have trouble, you have a refuge. God does not always do away with all of our troubles, but He always provides a refuge. We want the Lord to kill all of our Pharaohs. He did not tell Moses that he would kill Pharaoh, but He did promise that He would go with Moses to face Pharaoh. God is not going to get rid of all our trouble, but He will provide a refuge for us *"in times of trouble."*

124

If I did not have a refuge in all of these storms, I would be swept away! I praise His holy name that I have a refuge. His name is Jesus Christ! The Bible says in verse ten, *"And they that know thy name will put their trust in thee: for thou, LORD, hast not forsaken them that seek thee."* How are others going to know God's name unless we tell them?

> *God does not always do away with all of our troubles, but He always provides a refuge.*

I was driving through an area with my wife recently, and we stopped to talk to a man in his yard. In our conversation, I asked the man, "Are you a Christian?" He answered, "Well, I try to be. I want to be. I've been thinking about being one." Do you know what he needed? He needed someone to simply be specific with him and to tell him of the Savior. When we told him about the Lord and how Christ could save him, he bowed his head and asked God to forgive his sin and trusted the Lord Jesus as his Savior.

We must tell people His name and what He can do! It is not right for us to act like the rest of the world! It is not right for us to simply wring our hands, shake our heads, shed our tears, and surrender as if things are so terrible that we can do nothing! We must lift our voices and say, "Look, there is hope! His name is Jesus! Put your faith in Christ! Trust in the Lord." *"Declare among the people his doings"*

The Bible says in verse eleven, *"Sing praises to the LORD, which dwelleth in Zion: declare among the people his doings."* How many of us go through life without lifting our voice, without singing His praises, without talking about Christ? In the crowds, on the job, in the lunchroom, in the schoolroom, we must start talking about Him. I believe we could have a revival if people who know the Lord would just start talking about Him!

The Bible says, *"Praise his name" "Sing praises to the LORD."* There is a lot of difference between a singer who knows and loves the Lord and a singer who does not love the Lord. You can hear it in the song they sing!

GOD MAKES INQUISITION

Verse twelve says, *"When he maketh inquisition for blood, he remembereth them: he forgetteth not the cry of the humble."* God is going to put out a great inquiry someday! All the blood that has been shed, and all the secret things that have been done will be judged accordingly.

Three babies are aborted every minute in America. Those doctors may carry home a paycheck, but one day they are going to be on God's list. When He does the great inquiry, God knows who has shed innocent blood. People may have gotten by with things, and they may have even profited from what they have gotten by with in this life, but there is coming a day when the Judge of all the ages does His inquiring. We need to lift up a holy standard and preach about a righteous, sin-hating God that men might see that someday they are going to have to meet God.

The Bible says in verses twelve through thirteen, *"When he maketh inquisition for blood, he remembereth them: he forgetteth not the cry of the humble. Have mercy upon me, O LORD; consider my trouble which I suffer of them that hate me, thou that liftest me up from the gates of death."* David said, *"They are after me ; they are about to kill me, and I am suffering at their hands near the gates of death!"* But the Lord did not let him die! The Lord lifted him up from the gates of death so that he could show forth all God's praise in the gates of the daughter of Zion.

How many of God's children have been saved from the gates of death, yet have never gotten to the gates of Zion, praising the

Lord? You would not even know they are saved! There should be Christians praising God everywhere and lifting up His holy name. Oh, what a wonderful a Savior we have! We have been lifted up from the gates of death, and we should be at the gates of the daughter of Zion singing His praises.

David said, *"I will rejoice in thy salvation."* Think what we have! The Devil had you kidnapped and was running off to hell with you. No one could pay your ransom. But Christ came to ransom us! He paid the price with His own precious blood, and He redeemed us. He has justified us, He has adopted us, and He has given us the Holy Spirit. We are joint heirs with Christ! Think of all we have in salvation! We have a heavenly Guide living in us and abiding in us, the Holy Spirit. He is the Comforter who will never leave us or forsake us! We know that our last breath here will be our first breath in the presence of the Lord Jesus, and we will walk on streets of gold and see loved ones who have gone on before us and meet Christians we have heard about in history and saints we have read about in God's Word.

> *It is not right for us to simply wring our hands, shake our heads, shed our tears, and surrender as if things are so terrible that we can do nothing!*

David said, *"I will rejoice in thy salvation."* In verse fifteen, he says of the heathen, *"The heathen are sunk down in the pit that they made: in the net which they hid is their own foot taken."* Think of that! Sin makes a fool out of people. The Bible says, *"They make their own net."* They think they are going to get someone else, but they get caught themselves!

Verses fifteen and sixteen tell us, *"The heathen are sunk down in the pit that they made: in the net which they hid is their own foot taken. The LORD is known by the judgment which he executeth: the wicked is snared in the work of his own hands."* Then these words,

"Higgaion" and *"Selah,"* are given which mean "to tune" and "to think." "Don't get in a hurry," God says. "Think about this."

What do you want your employer to know? What do you want your wife to know, your children to know, your husband to know, your mother to know, your father to know? Everything the Devil likes for you to do in secret will be broadcast to all those people someday! Sin makes a fool out of you!

How many of God's children have been saved from the gates of death, yet have never gotten to the gates of Zion, praising the Lord?

The Bible says in Psalm 9:17-19, *"The wicked shall be turned into hell, and all the nations that forget God. For the needy shall not alway be forgotten: the expectation of the poor shall not perish for ever. Arise, O LORD; let not man prevail: let the heathen be judged in thy sight."* Exodus 14:30-31 records that when Pharaoh took off with his armies after the children of Israel, God judged them. The bodies of those thousands of Egyptians floated in the Red Sea before the faces of the Israelites. Read it for yourself! They witnessed the judgment of God.

We read in Psalm 9:20, *"Put them in fear, O LORD: that the nations may know themselves to be but men."* How we exalt people! How we attach fame to people! Because of the beauty God gave them, they are exalted. They do not need anyone. Because of athletic abilities that some people are blessed with and have developed, they are given millions and millions of dollars. Even in churches, people are exalted. On the job, people are exalted. Do you know what you and I need? We need to know that we are merely men.

The psalmist prayed, "Lord, let the people know; let them see themselves to be but men." That is all. When you do see yourself this way, you will seek the Lord for help. When you see yourself as exalted, powerful, manipulative, winsome, able, beautiful, it is dangerous. We must pray, "Lord, help us to see ourselves to be but men who need Thee and who need to trust the Lord Jesus for our salvation. As Christians, we must trust the Lord each day for the grace and strength we need to live the Christian life."

PSALM 10:1-4

Why standest thou afar off, O LORD? why hidest thou thyself in times of trouble?

The wicked in his pride doth persecute the poor: let them be taken in the devices that they have imagined.

For the wicked boasteth of his heart's desire, and blesseth the covetous, whom the LORD abhorreth.

The wicked, through the pride of his countenance, will not seek after God: God is not in all his thoughts.

 e find a very descriptive account of the wicked in the tenth Psalm. The Bible says in verse one, *"Why standest thou afar off, O LORD? why hidest thou thyself in times of trouble?"* All of us know what trouble is, some to a greater degree than others. The Bible speaks here of *"times of trouble."* The word used for trouble in this first verse refers to trouble with people, not trouble with things or with health, but trouble with people.

Consider Your Salvation

The psalmist says, *"Why standest thou afar off, O LORD? why hidest thou thyself in times of trouble?"* When trouble comes to the believer the first thing to do is consider your salvation. If you are a child of God, nothing and no one can take your salvation from you. The Lord Jesus said in John 10:27-29,

> *My sheep hear my voice, and I know them, and*
> *they follow me. And I give unto them eternal life; and*

they shall never perish, neither shall any man pluck them out of my hand. My Father, which gave them me, is greater than all; and no man is able to pluck them out of my Father's hand.

Develop a Grateful Heart

The second bit of advice I have for you is to develop a grateful heart. Work on having a grateful heart. The first thing we are tempted to do when going through trouble is to start counting our miseries and woes. Satan begins to work on our mind. He wants us to think that God has not been good to us. He knows the goodness of God leads to repentance. Ingratitude becomes a garden from which all kinds of evil fruit grow.

Seek Counsel From God

When you are having trouble, the tendency is to run from the Lord. Instead, run to the Lord. Decide that you are going to move toward the Lord. How does God speak to us? He speaks to us through His Word. He speaks to us through prayer. He speaks to us through other believers. He speaks to us through the circumstances we go through.

Listen for God's Voice

Read your Bible. God will speak to you in your time of trouble. Listen for His voice, then look for the Lord Jesus in your trouble. As you seek Him, you will find Him. Look for Christ in your trouble.

THE WORLD IN WHICH WE LIVE

At first glance, it appears to our world that God has withdrawn Himself. There are some people who take the position that God started this world and then withdrew Himself from it.

The world in which we live is a world of trouble. In Psalm 10:1, the psalmist speaks to God concerning this trouble, *"Why standest thou afar off, O LORD? why hidest thou thyself in times of trouble?"* God is real, and God is able. But the psalmist says, "It seems to me as if God is not near."

Not long ago while traveling by plane, I was witnessing to a man and trying to get him to recognize his need to trust Christ as Savior. He said to me, "I have a problem with what is going on in the world." I said, "What do you mean?" I knew what was coming. He said, "If there really is a God who can do all things, why doesn't God do some things that need to be done?" He started naming things on his short list. I am sure he had a long one, but he gave me the short version of his list. He talked about some of the problems that he thought should be corrected, and he wondered why God did not step in and do something. Many people are hung up on this kind of thinking.

Satan uses the world to pollute; God uses trouble in the world to purge us.

We are living in a world in which there is terrible trouble. Often, we do not see this trouble until God seems to have withdrawn from us. *"Why standest thou afar off, O LORD? why hidest thou thyself in times of trouble?"* Let us gain insight about how God uses the world, this world in which we live.

He uses the world as a purging influence on His children, not a polluting influence. Satan uses the world to pollute; God uses trouble in the world to purge us. It is all in the way we respond to the work of Christ in our own personal lives as we are dealing with things in this world.

We will come back to the tenth Psalm, but let us consider something in the New Testament book of John, the seventeenth chapter. We often call this the high priestly prayer of Jesus Christ. Why did He pray this way? Notice the last verse in John chapter sixteen. The Bible says in verse thirty-three, *"These things I have spoken unto you, that in me ye might have peace. In the world ye shall have tribulation: but be of good cheer; I have overcome the world."*

God is not trying to destroy us by allowing trouble. He is building us. Notice part of this prayer. The Bible says in John 17:14-15,

> *I have given them thy word; and the world hath hated them, because they are not of the world, even as I am not of the world. I pray not that thou shouldest take them out of the world, but that thou shouldest keep them from the evil.*

After coming to know the Lord Jesus Christ as Savior, He could take us to heaven immediately, but He does not work that way. He leaves us here in this world. The Bible says in verses sixteen and seventeen, *"They are not of the world, even as I am not of the world. Sanctify them through thy truth: thy word is truth."*

The word *"trouble"* in Psalm ten has to do with trouble concerning people, and it comes from a root word meaning "narrow" or "pressed." We might imagine an impossible passage. "I am not going to make it. It is too tough. I am going down in this one. It is too narrow for me." Why does God allow these things to come into our lives? Is the Lord interested in simply crushing the life out of us? No. But He is greatly concerned about purging the dross from us. He is interested in getting the things out of us that do not belong in a God-glorifying Christian. He can use the world as sandpaper to get the rough edges off our lives. We are left in the world to witness to others concerning the world to come. Also, God is conforming us to the image of His Son while we are in this world.

We need to look at the things that come to us (and I use the Bible word *"troubles"*) as things God gives to us in order to help us. When dealt with properly in the spirit of Jesus Christ, they make us more like our Lord.

Consider the fourteenth chapter of the book of Job. The Bible says in verse one, *"Man that is born of a woman is of few days, and full of trouble."* You cannot get out of this life without trouble. It is a part of life. God's grace is sufficient for all we face in life.

I was riding along with one of our men, a man that I love very much, and he said to me, "Sometimes you would just like to hold your children at a certain age and enjoy them at that age and not let them get to another step in life. It is so wonderful right where it is." I understand what he meant by that.

> *We are left in the world to witness to others concerning the world to come.*

My response to him was this: as a grown man, I have gone through some things that I would not have chosen for myself, but God has taught me about Himself and brought much joy to my life through my children, through their wives, through my grandchildren, through friendships, through difficulties and trials. God has brought things into my life from my childhood to this moment which have been so meaningful and so precious and so wonderful. From my perspective, yes, it might have been good to hold them in a certain stage of life and keep them at that stage for the rest of their lives. But truly, to enjoy the best and blessed life, they ought to have the privilege to grow and develop and learn of the Lord as we have learned of the Lord, that He is wonderful and that He never fails.

As a young teen I went through the death of a parent and a broken home. As a Christian, one does not say, "You know, I have been in a broken home. I know what that is like." No, you should say, "I have gone through a broken home and God took me through it. He cared for me." You do not say, "I have lost a parent. I know what that is like." No, you say, "I have been to the grave of a parent, and God went there with me, and He strengthened me and encouraged me."

I can look back now across these many years and talk about some things God has helped me through that I could not talk about as a teenager. Trouble? Yes. Trouble with people? Yes. The world in which we live is a world of trouble, but God has never failed me. At that time, I thought I could not get through. I thought the passage was too narrow. I thought I could not make it, but by His grace I did. You will too. When you get through, you will say, "It was by God's grace that I made it."

Let me give a little precious passage, also from the book of Job, on this same subject. The Bible says in Job 23:1-6,

> *Then Job answered and said, Even to day is my complaint bitter: my stroke is heavier than my groaning. Oh that I knew where I might find him! that I might come even to his seat! I would order my cause before him, and fill my mouth with arguments. I would know the words which he would answer me, and understand what he would say unto me. Will he plead against me with his great power? No; but he would put strength in me.*

Job is saying, "I am under such a load. I am groaning. I am complaining. The truth is, the stroke that I have received is heavier than my groaning. Where is God? I want to run to his seat. Where is He?" God's Word continues in verses seven through nine,

> *There the righteous might dispute with him; so should I be delivered for ever from my judge. Behold, I go forward, but he is not there; and backward, but I cannot perceive him: On the left hand, where he doth work, but I cannot behold him: he hideth himself on the right hand, that I cannot see him.*

This sounds like Psalm ten and verse one. *"Why standest thou afar off, O LORD?"* Verse ten of Job twenty-three is a verse that leaps off the page directly into your heart, *"But he knoweth the way that I take: when he hath tried me, I shall come forth as gold."* Job said, "I can't find Him, but He always knows where I am." There are times–moments, days, maybe weeks or even months–when it seems as if God is further away than you ever thought He could be or would be. I want you to tell you that He knows right where you are. He knows exactly what you are going through. *"He knoweth the way that I take."*

THE WICKED WITH WHICH WE DEAL

The world in which we live is a world of trouble. Let us look secondly at the wicked with which we deal. Some of the old authors, when presenting this tenth Psalm, called it the "Psalm of the Antichrist." Beginning with verse two down through verse eleven, they declared this to be a description of the antichrist. Let us look at the wicked with which we deal.

Every time the words *"the wicked"* appear, they ought to be noted. Every time God gives us something descriptive about the wicked in

His Word–the ways of the wicked or something about the wicked–it ought to be noted.

Persecute the Poor

Verse two says, *"The wicked in his pride doth persecute the poor."* *"The poor"* does not simply mean people who have no money. The word *"poor"* here means those who are needy, those who appear to have no one to help them in their need. It is as though they are prey for the wicked. *"The wicked in his pride..."* Notice how God starts. Where does this wickedness come from? It comes from a proud heart; does it not?

Boasteth of His Heart's Desire

The description continues in verse three, *"For the wicked boasteth of his heart's desire, and blesseth the covetous, whom the LORD abhorreth."* He said that the wicked boasts about what he desires in his heart, and he does exactly the opposite of what God would have him to do. He brags on those that we should be preaching against. *"For the wicked boasteth of his heart's desire."*

Will Not Seek After God

We read in the fourth verse, *"The wicked, through the pride of his countenance, will not seek after God: God is not in all his thoughts."* The wicked man will not seek after God. He has consciously made the decision to reject God. God says that the wicked man, having his thoughts examined, has no thought of God.

Ways Are Grievous

Verse five declares, *"His ways are always grievous; thy judgments are far above out of his sight: as for all his enemies, he puffeth at them."* The wicked man is full of himself. He is puffed up. The Bible says his ways are always grievous and nothing brings joy or delight.

The judgments of God are out of his sight. The fact that there is a God to answer to does not cross his mind. He *"puffeth"* at all of his enemies. He is simply full of himself.

Shall Not Be Moved

Verse six says, *"He hath said in his heart, I shall not be moved: for I shall never be in adversity."* In his heart, the seat of emotion, he says, "I am never going to be changed. I am never going move. I shall never be in adversity. I am going to live as I please, think as I please, do anything I please to do. I am going to take the reins and throw them to the wind and do exactly what I feel like doing." That is the wicked. We are living in that kind of world. These wicked people are the people with which we must deal.

There is a real heaven and a real hell. They may live this way, but when they die, they are going to go to hell forever. When we die, we are going to heaven forever if we know the Lord Jesus as our Savior.

Mouth Full of Cursing

The Bible says in verse seven, *"His mouth is full of cursing and deceit and fraud: under his tongue is mischief and vanity."* We see his ways, his heart, his cursing and deceitful mouth. He cannot tell the truth and will not tell the truth. *"His tongue is mischief and vanity."* What is not deceitful and mischievous is vain and empty.

Sitteth in Lurking Places

Again we read in verse eight, *"He sitteth in the lurking places of the villages: in the secret places doth he murder the innocent: his eyes are privily set against the poor."* He slips around secretly, behind the scenes, putting an end to life that is precious and beautiful. He is a murderer of the innocent.

139

Imagine a girl or a young man that could have been something beautiful and decent and holy and God-fearing, but some wicked beast got to her or to him and introduced wickedness to that young person. This is murdering the innocent, stealing their innocence. I understand that people of their own volition yield to sin, but there are wicked people seeking to corrupt others, seducing them into sin, preying on people.

I think about all the precious young people who come to our Christian school and our Christian college. They are not all what they ought to be, but they represent as fine a group of people as can be found anywhere in the world. Do you not know that there are out there in places where they go and work, places where they might visit, wicked people who are waiting to attempt to take whatever innocence they have from them.

We live in that kind of wicked world, and it is filled with wicked people. God did not take us out of it. He left us in it. He did not leave us here to punish us. We are to be salt and light. We will have a purging influence in this world if we keep our eyes on Christ and remove our feet from the path that leads to evil things, fleeing as Joseph fled at the first mention or thought of wickedness.

There are those who come to Christ from a life of terrible sin. God makes them whole, washes them in His precious blood, and speaks to their heart in some Bible-believing, Bible-preaching church. They say that God has led them, God has called them, and God has brought them, and some devil is waiting to attempt to mislead them. We need to hold them up before the Lord in prayer.

The Bible says of the wicked in verses eight and nine,

> *He sitteth in the lurking places of the villages: in the secret places doth he murder the innocent: his eyes are privily set against the poor. He lieth in wait secretly as a lion in his den: he lieth in wait to catch*

*the poor: he doth catch the poor, when he draweth
him into his net.*

He has already set the trap and is waiting to get them. *"He
croucheth, and humbleth himself, that the poor may fall by his strong
ones."* Like a beast, he is ready to pounce on his prey.

Accuses God

Verse eleven says, *"He hath said in his heart, God hath forgotten:
he hideth his face; he will never see it."* The wicked say, "I don't have
to worry about God. I don't have to worry about getting caught. Look
what I have done. Look how I have lived. I have lived as I pleased.
I have done what I wanted to do. God has never stopped me; He is
not going to stop me now." This is the way the wicked talk. They
become bolder and bolder in their wickedness. You know where they
are headed; do you not? They are headed to hell and destruction.

This is the kind of world in which we live, and this is the kind
of wickedness and wicked people with which we deal. Think of
this—*"God hath forgotten."* If you start talking to them about the
Lord, they say, "I've lived like this for fifteen years, twenty years,
thirty years, forty years. He hasn't caught me yet, has He?" They are
headed to a sudden destruction.

THE WORK OF THE LORD

We have seen the world in which we live and the wicked with
which we deal. The third thing we must consider is the work of the
Lord. The Bible says in verse twelve, *"Arise, O LORD; O God, lift up
thine hand: forget not the humble."* What does God do in response
to all this? He lifts His hand.

We had a teacher years ago who taught in our elementary school, and she had the greatest discipline in her class I have witnessed. My idea of an elementary school teacher is a sergeant with compassion. This lady exemplified so much of what I love to see in a teacher. When she wanted her class to do something, she would raise her hand. When she raised her hand, there was not a sound made, and every eye was on her. Every child in the class knew immediately, "We are under her authority. She is in control."

The psalmist says, "Lift your hand." And God lifts His hand. That is His work. That is enough. One of these days, God is going to lift His hand and say, "That is enough." I have faith in the One who can lift His hand and say, "That is enough."

The Bible says that God does not forget. His work is not to forget. He chooses to forget our sins and our transgressions. Isaiah 38:17 says, *"Behold, for peace I had great bitterness: but thou hast in love to my soul delivered it from the pit of corruption: for thou hast cast all my sins behind thy back."* He buries our sins in the sea of forgetfulness. God forgets our sins, but the Bible says He will not forget the humble.

Verse thirteen says, *"Wherefore doth the wicked contemn God?"* This means to despise or to scorn God. Can you imagine someone despising or scorning God? *"He hath said in his heart, Thou wilt not require it."* In other words, "I have done as I pleased, and God is never going to bring me to judgment." This is not true.

Verse fourteen says, *"Thou hast seen it: for thou beholdest mischief and spite, to requite it with thy hand: the poor committeth himself unto thee; thou art the helper of the fatherless."* God says that His work is to bring people to judgment. The wicked say, "God is never going to get me." And God says, "Oh, yes, I am going to get you."

The fifteenth verse says, *"Break thou the arm of the wicked."* People get puffed up and think they can do anything and get by with it. The psalmist prays for God to break their arms, meaning to destroy their strength and their ability to do anything. Do you remember the Bible says in the Revelation of Jesus Christ that kings, great men of the earth, are going to cry for the rocks to fall on them?

Do you remember the apostle Paul wrote in the book of Philippians that every knee will bow and every tongue confess that Jesus Christ is Lord to the glory of God the Father? There is a great humbling coming. Our God is the One who will humble men. It will be too late. *"Seek out his wickedness till thou find none."* Do you know what this means? God is going to bring them all in. In God's great search, He will uncover everything. No stone will be left unturned when God is finished. He is thorough.

Then right in the middle of this, the Bible says in verse sixteen, *"The LORD is King for ever and ever: the heathen are perished out of his land."* Is that not a great expression? The psalm then concludes, *"LORD, thou hast heard the desire of the humble: thou wilt prepare their heart, thou wilt cause thine ear to hear: to judge the fatherless and the oppressed, that the man of the earth may no more oppress."* This is what God does.

Have you had to deal with some of this wicked behavior? Does it seem to you that God is a little late arriving to do something about the situation? Many would say yes. So what are we to do? We are to put our faith and confidence in God that He will do what only He can do in His time. Do not be shaken. He may seem to be far off in times of trouble, but there is not doubt that He will be faithful to accomplish His work in His time.

143

Psalm 11

In the LORD *put I my trust: how say ye to my soul, Flee as a bird to your mountain?*

For, lo, the wicked bend their bow, they make ready their arrow upon the string, that they may privily shoot at the upright in heart.

If the foundations be destroyed, what can the righteous do?

The LORD is in his holy temple, the LORD's throne is in heaven: his eyes behold, his eyelids try, the children of men.

The LORD trieth the righteous: but the wicked and him that loveth violence his soul hateth.

Upon the wicked he shall rain snares, fire and brimstone, and an horrible tempest: this shall be the portion of their cup.

For the righteous LORD loveth righteousness; his countenance doth behold the upright.

CHAPTER ELEVEN

IF THE FOUNDATIONS BE DESTROYED

hings are not always what they appear to be. We can be deceived if we are not trusting the Lord to give us discernment and wisdom. Charles Haddon Spurgeon called the eleventh Psalm "The Psalm of the Steadfast"; it is the psalm of those who will not be moved. There are times when it appears as if the foundations have been destroyed. Do not be troubled. It only appears to be so. We read in Psalm 11:3, *"If the foundations be destroyed, what can the righteous do?"*

Most people agree that the setting for this psalm took place when David was in the palace with Saul. He was a young man playing his harp to soothe the troubled king. Under the attack that came to David from Saul, friends advised him to flee, but he did not run, at least not then. He waited on the Lord and His direction.

When David said, *"If the foundations be destroyed,"* he must have felt very discouraged. He beheld the king of Israel, on whose throne and in whose palace everything should have been right, but things

145

were not right. The psalmist cried, *"If the foundations be destroyed, what can the righteous do?"*

At the close of the third chapter of the Revelation of Jesus Christ, the church is gone from the earth. Chapters two and three of the Revelation deal with the church age. However, in chapter four and verse one, we find something very interesting. The Bible says, *"After this I looked, and, behold, a door was opened in heaven: and the first voice which I heard was as it were of a trumpet talking with me; which said, Come up hither, and I will shew thee things which must be hereafter."*

If you are familiar with the Revelation of Jesus Christ, you know that as the book progresses, we move back and forth from earth to heaven. As God gives us a glimpse into heaven in this fourth chapter, the Bible says in verse two, *"And immediately I was in the spirit: and, behold, a throne was set in heaven, and one sat on the throne."*

This is God's throne. He is still on the throne. We are in the church age, and God revealed to John that when the church age is finished, He will still be on the throne. We may get the idea at times that the Lord has forsaken us or has forsaken this planet and that everything that can go wrong is going wrong. It appears as if all the foundations have been destroyed, but the Bible says when we come to the end of this age, God will still be on the throne. If God is still on the throne when it is all over, then we must realize that God is still on the throne at this very moment. The reins of the universe are still in the hands of Almighty God.

THE DANGER WE FACE

We understand that there is a perceived danger. There is also a real danger. Often we do not recognize the real danger, but it is easily seen in this eleventh Psalm. The Bible says concerning the danger we face in Psalm 11:1-2, *"In the LORD put I my trust: how say ye to my soul, Flee as a bird to your mountain? For, lo, the wicked bend their bow, they make ready their arrow upon the string, that they may privily shoot at the upright in heart."*

Notice the word picture given. The enemy has his bow in hand. The arrow is on the string. The bow is drawn. He is about to let the arrow fly and pierce David's heart.

The dangers that David faced in the court of Saul are given to us here in composite form. Because of all the things that looked so dangerous coming from the hand of Saul, David had to decide either to flee because of fear or to have faith in God.

We perceive that the greatest danger is what we see—the enemy, whoever that enemy may be. The enemy with bow drawn, words spoken, and with evil intent in his heart, has every idea of harming you. You cannot reason with him. You cannot communicate with him.

Saul was like a mad man. There was no way to reason with him. The perceived danger was from the hand of Saul, but that was not the real danger. The real danger was not the danger David faced from Saul. The real danger was that as David faced Saul's anger, he would get out of the will of God. The real danger is not facing the enemy. The real danger is in failing to trust the Lord when facing the enemy.

> *The reins of the universe are still in the hands of Almighty God.*

Where can you go to escape trouble? Remember, the Bible says in Job 14:1, *"Man that is born of a woman is of few days, and full of trouble."* How can you raise a family and occasionally not have trouble to deal with? We perceive the danger to be the people or circumstances that threaten to harm us, but that is not the greatest danger. The greatest danger is the danger of failing to trust God when facing the enemy.

When someone is having trouble with their children or having some problem at their work place, I understand their grief, but that is not the kind of thing that brings about our downfall. Our downfall comes when we do not trust God in the midst of what we are facing.

> *The real danger is not facing the enemy. The real danger is in failing to trust the Lord when facing the enemy.*

David's temptation was not to take another spear in hand and kill Saul. That would have temporarily taken care of the trouble, but it would not have solved anything. We want the Lord to rid us of all our Sauls. If it had not been Saul, it would have been someone else. The temptation was to flee. Eventually David did flee, but he left at God's direction and in God's timing. In this psalm he said, *"In the LORD put I my trust: how say ye to my soul, Flee as a bird to your mountain?"*

There is no life without trouble and difficulty. The next time you think, "I am having a hard time, and this person is giving me a hard time," realize that trouble is not the most dangerous thing. The most dangerous thing is the temptation to run from it and not run to the Lord for strength to carry on.

THE DELIVERANCE WE HAVE

The Bible says in Psalm 11:3-4, *"If the foundations be destroyed, what can the righteous do? The LORD is in his holy temple, the LORD's throne is in heaven: his eyes behold, his eyelids try, the children of men."*

"If the foundations be destroyed, what can the righteous do?" If what we are counting on, what we believe in, what we hope for, what

we are trusting in is destroyed, what can we do? In other words, if what we are standing on falls, where can we stand?

For example, someone may go to the doctor thinking his health is fine, only to hear the doctor say after the examination, "You have cancer." That person may think, "My life is ruined." No, he still has a life. If he has the Lord Jesus, he still has a home in heaven. He still has all eternity before him. He still has a Savior. He still has a foundation.

I have counseled many people in my lifetime who have said, "My family is gone, and my life is ruined. My home is broken." These things are extremely difficult and very painful. These people say, "The foundation is destroyed." It may appear that way, but they still have a life. If they are Christians, they still have a Savior. They still have a future. They still have forgiveness. They still have God.

It does not matter that the king did not do right. Oh, I wish he had, but he didn't. God is still on the throne. He is our deliverance. Did you know that there is a foundation that cannot be moved? The Bible says in I Corinthians 3:11, *"For other foundation can no man lay than that is laid, which is Jesus Christ."*

How do you destroy that foundation? Christ cannot be destroyed! The Bible says in II Timothy 2:15-19,

> *Study to shew thyself approved unto God, a workman that needeth not to be ashamed, rightly dividing the word of truth. But shun profane and vain babblings: for they will increase unto more ungodliness.*

Take heed to this. Notice where some people are headed. We must obey God by shunning profane and vain babblings. You say, "It is not so bad," but the Bible says it will get worse. Verse sixteen continues,

> *...for they will increase unto more ungodliness. And their word will eat as doth a canker: of whom*

is Hymenaeus and Philetus; who concerning the truth have erred, saying that the resurrection is past already; and overthrow the faith of some.

Can you imagine being in church with Hymenaeus and Philetus? Can you imagine this erupting in the church assembly? Imagine the pain it caused. Can you imagine someone saying, "It is destroyed; it is gone"? No, it just appears that way, because the Bible says in verse nineteen,

> *Nevertheless the foundation of God standeth sure, having this seal, the Lord knoweth them that are his. And, let every one that nameth the name of Christ depart from iniquity.*

There are so many times in life when it looks as though the bottom has fallen out, but it was not the bottom. It just looked like the bottom. The bottom is Jesus Christ, and He is not going to fall out. He is our foundation. The hymn writer declared the truth when he wrote, "On Christ the solid Rock I stand, all other ground in sinking sand!"

David learned a great lesson. He said, "The danger is that Saul is trying to kill me. Surely it is going to happen." His friends told him, "Run from him. Flee as a bird. Go to the mountains." David said, "No, I am not going to do that. I am going to stay here until God tells me to go. I am going to trust the Lord. The real danger is not Saul. The real danger is in not trusting God." His friends said, "The foundations are destroyed. Even the king and his throne are corrupt." It did look that way, but the Bible says in verse four that *"the LORD's throne is in heaven."* Even though Saul was not doing what he should have done on his earthly throne, God was doing what He should have been doing on His heavenly throne. It only appeared that the foundation was gone. This was David's deliverance, not the arm of flesh.

In the Gospel according to Luke we see this illustrated. In the eighth chapter, the Lord Jesus had been in the land of Gadara, and the Gadarene maniac had believed on Him. This man had been a wild man, naked and mad. They tried to chain him, and he had such demonic power, he could break the chains. Can you imagine a man like that running loose? What would you do? You would lock your doors, bolt everything down, and keep your family inside.

The Lord Jesus met the man and changed his life. If he lived in your neighborhood, this would be great news to you. Christ cast the demons out of that Gadarene maniac. The demons entered into the hogs, and the hogs ran violently over a cliff into the sea. The owners said to the Lord Jesus, "Get out of town; we don't want you here."

The Lord Jesus crossed the sea and came over to the other side, where a man met him. He was a ruler of the synagogue, and he said, "I have one daughter. She is twelve years old, and she is dying." The Lord Jesus started out with him, and as He went, a woman came pressing through the crowd. This woman had an issue of blood for twelve years. She touched the hem of His garment. He stopped everything, got the woman's attention,

God allows us to fail so we learn to trust in Him.

and told her that her faith in Him had made her whole. It was not the garment, but her faith that made her whole. Then the Bible says in Luke 8:49, *"While he yet spake, there cometh one from the ruler of the synagogue's house, saying to him, Thy daughter is dead; trouble not the Master."*

They said, "It is too late. She's dead." In other words, they said that there is a limit to what the Lord Jesus could do. If she was sick, He could touch her body and restore her health, but now they did not believe there was anything He could do. They thought, "The girl is dead; tell the master He can go home. The foundation is destroyed. It is fallen through. Now it is ended, and it will never work out."

The Lord Jesus went on to the house. He went into the room and said, "She is not dead. She is sleeping." She was dead, but He was illustrating a point. The Bible says that they *"laughed him to scorn."* Then He raised the girl from the dead.

I have not seen any dead people brought back to life, but I want to make this application. There are many times when we think because something bad has happened, and it has gotten even worse, that our lives are over and finished. We all have lines drawn that testify to what point we are willing to believe God. May God help us, by faith, to erase these limiting lines.

I heard a pastor speak when I was twenty years old. He wept and cried at a church in Nashville, Tennessee. He asked the people gathered there to pray for him. He had followed his young son through the streets. The boy, full of drugs, turned on him and was going to kill him. The dad said, "I can hardly live under this load. If it were not for God, if it were not for my faith in God, I could not stand here today."

I thought, "How in this world can anything like that ever happen to someone in the ministry?" Twenty years later I saw the same pastor in a restaurant. I walked up to him and said, "Twenty years ago I heard you say that you had followed your son through the streets of your city. You finally found him, and I heard you weep and ask everyone to pray for you and him. We all prayed. Twenty years later, I must ask, where is your son?" He said, "Thank God, today he is my assistant pastor."

At times, it looks as if the foundation is gone, but there is something below that. It is the foundation of God which standeth sure.

David said, "Oh, it looks like all of Israel is in an uproar. It looks like God's kingdom is gone. It looks like everything is torn apart. It looks like the foundation is destroyed. But the Lord is still on His throne in heaven."

Do you remember the story of Lazarus? He was dead four days. His sister met the Lord Jesus and said, "If You had been here, he wouldn't have died, but You are here too late." The foundation seemed to be gone. There seemed to be no hope, but Christ raised him from the dead. We must understand that our deliverance is in the Lord. Oh, friends, as we trust in men, God allows us to fail so we learn to trust in Him.

THE DESIGN GOD HAS FOR OUR LIVES

Why does God allow these things to happen? Some people have a mental picture of the Lord up in heaven getting some sort of thrill out of watching people suffer. I know that in many cases sin brings the human suffering we see, but there are a lot of people hurting, and no one can explain the reason for all their pain.

What does God have for our lives? Notice what the psalm says in verses five and six, *"The LORD trieth the righteous: but the wicked and him that loveth violence his soul hateth. Upon the wicked he shall rain snares, fire and brimstone, and an horrible tempest: this shall be the portion of their cup."*

In other words, what the wicked have is destruction. What about the righteous? God tries the righteous. We read in verse seven, *"For the righteous LORD loveth righteousness; his countenance doth behold the upright."*

What do you love? The Bible says, *"The righteous LORD loveth righteousness."* God's design is not to destroy us. God's design is not to hurt us. God's design is to produce righteous living in us. He loves righteousness.

We often complain about what we have to deal with and what we have to go through and end up praying, "Lord, I have had enough. I cannot go any further or do anything else. Lord, you are going to have to help me. Come to my rescue. Strengthen me. Hold me up." In that moment of looking by faith to God, He strengthens us to continue.

> *God's design is not to destroy us. God's design is not to hurt us. God's design is to produce righteous living in us.*

David thought dealing with Saul was difficult. Perhaps he thought playing his harp before the king was a difficult task, but one day he would be on the throne and leading an entire nation. God was training David to trust Him.

Sometimes I think, "I am the boss; I am in charge; I have so much to do." I run around like the director, putting all the pieces in place. God helping me, instead of trying to do things right, I want to do the right things more and more. The Bible says in Psalm 11:4, *"His eyes behold, his eyelids try, the children of men."*

The figure of speech used here speaks of the fact that God squints His eyes so that everything else is out of focus, and I am His focus. He looks on me. This is what He is doing. He is building you and me.

Do you think your foundation is destroyed? It is not. We have one Foundation that can never be moved. That Foundation is Jesus Christ! If you do not know the Lord Jesus Christ as your personal Savior, trust Him now. He paid your sin debt. He rose from the dead. He is alive today. Ask Him to forgive your sin. Invite Him into your life. Build your life on the Lord Jesus Christ.

PSALM 12

Help, LORD; for the godly man ceaseth; for the faithful fail from among the children of men.

They speak vanity every one with his neighbour: with flattering lips and with a double heart do they speak.

The LORD shall cut off all flattering lips, and the tongue that speaketh proud things:

Who have said, With our tongue will we prevail; our lips are our own: who is lord over us?

For the oppression of the poor, for the sighing of the needy, now will I arise, saith the LORD; I will set him in safety from him that puffeth at him.

The words of the LORD are pure words: as silver tried in a furnace of earth, purified seven times.

Thou shalt keep them, O LORD, thou shalt preserve them from this generation for ever.

The wicked walk on every side, when the vilest men are exalted.

CHAPTER TWELVE

HELP, LORD

o you know the Lord Jesus as your Savior? Do you know heaven is your home? I hope you do. I hope there is no doubt in your mind that Jesus Christ is your Savior and heaven is your home.

In Psalm twelve, we find in the first verse that the psalmist David was considering what was going on *"among the children of men."* The background of this particular psalm took place in the life of David when he was fleeing the wrath of Saul.

In the city of Nob, David had been to see Ahimelech the priest. As David went there to find refuge and food, an Edomite by the name of Doeg spied on David. He saw the priest give David bread and the sword of Goliath. David later went on to the cave of Adullam where hundreds of people joined him.

Saul heard about what had happened in the city of Nob, and in his anger, he ordered that all the priests in that city be killed. Saul's men would not kill them. But Doeg, who reported that David had received

aid from these priests, was willing to kill them. He not only killed all the priests in that city, all these men of God, but he also killed all the children, all the women, all the babies that were nursing, and all the animals in that city of priests.

> *Perhaps there are no two words in the Bible that express the depth of human need and the heighth of hope any more than these two words, "Help, LORD."*

No doubt David felt tremendously responsible for what had happened. He knew when Doeg had seen him that some trouble was going to come of it. David writes in this psalm about the godly ceasing from the earth and the faithful failing from the children of men.

The psalmist said in verse one, *"Help, LORD; for the godly man ceaseth; for the faithful fail from among the children of men."* The godly are ceasing; the faithful are failing. What is going on *"among the children of men"*? Do you ever get the idea that in the world in which we live, the wicked are winning?

Perhaps there are no two words in the Bible that express the depth of human need and the heighth of hope any more than these two words, *"Help, LORD."* How many times in our lives have we tried to get people to see their need, and they have seen their need, but they have failed to see their only hope is in the Lord? However, when we recognize our need and cry out to God, then we witness what God alone can accomplish in our lives.

This twelfth Psalm says,

> *Help, LORD; for the godly man ceaseth; for the faithful fail from among the children of men. They speak vanity every one with his neighbour: with flattering lips and with a double heart do they speak. The LORD shall cut off all flattering lips, and the tongue*

that speaketh proud things: who have said, With our tongue will we prevail; our lips are our own: who is lord over us? For the oppression of the poor, for the sighing of the needy, now will I arise, saith the LORD; I will set him in safety from him that puffeth at him. The words of the LORD are pure words: as silver tried in a furnace of earth, purified seven times. Thou shalt keep them, O LORD, thou shalt preserve them from this generation for ever. The wicked walk on every side, when the vilest men are exalted.

The reason we are seeing and hearing of so much wickedness today is that vile men have been exalted. When vile men are exalted, the world is filled with wickedness. Verse eight says, *"The wicked walk on every side, when the vilest men are exalted."*

We live in an age of bold wickedness. We witness daily the flaunting of evil. The blush is gone. The Bible says there is a reason for this. *"The wicked walk on every side, when the vilest men are exalted."*

You make of it what you will, but I am concerned about our children and our grandchildren. Where are we to turn for help?

OUR HELP IS IN GOD

The Bible says, *"Help, LORD."* The Word of God says in verse five, *"For the oppression of the poor, for the sighing of the needy, now will I arise, saith the LORD."* What we must have in this country is a crying out to God for help and a sighing of the needy that will stir the Lord to arise and do something in our land. Our help is in the Lord. We ought to be crying out to God.

In the book of Habakkuk, we see this illustrated. Habakkuk was living on the eve of the captivity of the nation of Judah. The

Babylonians were about to march down and take the southern kingdom of Judah. There was great trouble in the land. The trouble was not that the Babylonians were coming; it was that God's people had forsaken the Lord.

The real heart of the problem in our nation is not the vile, wicked people we hear; it is the silence of God's people. This is a day to rise up and do something. Rise up and speak the truth. Let your voice be heard. I find myself going from place to place trying to rally people to rise up and speak out about what they believe. The prophet says in Habakkuk 1:1-4,

The reason we are seeing and hearing of so much wickedness today is that vile men have been exalted.

The burden which Habakkuk the prophet did see. O LORD, how long shall I cry, and thou wilt not hear! even cry out unto thee of violence, and thou wilt not save! Why dost thou shew me iniquity, and cause me to behold grievance? for spoiling and violence are before me: and there are that raise up strife and contention. Therefore the law is slacked, and judgment doth never go forth: for the wicked doth compass about the righteous; therefore wrong judgment proceedeth.

He said, "It seems to me that the wicked are winning." *"The wicked doth compass about the righteous; therefore wrong judgment proceedeth."* Think of what kind of judgment is going to come to our nation as we adopt the vilest of lifestyles as ordinary and commonplace.

Notice how Habakkuk finally prays in Habakkuk 3:1-2, *"A prayer of Habakkuk the prophet upon Shigionoth. O LORD, I have heard thy speech, and was afraid: O LORD, revive thy work in the midst of the years, in the midst of the years make known; in wrath remember mercy."*

He prayed to God for revival. The only hope for our nation is a real heaven-sent revival. Let us set aside times in the life of our church when we open our buildings and ask Christians to come and pray, seeking God for revival. This is our only hope.

OUR HELP IS IN GOD'S WORD

The Bible says in Psalm 12:2 that these wicked people speak. *"They speak vanity every one with his neighbour: with flattering lips and with a double heart do they speak."* A double heart is hypocrisy. There are many double hearts and double tongues in this world.

The Bible says in verses three and four, *"The LORD shall cut off all flattering lips, and the tongue that speaketh proud things: who have said, With our tongue will we prevail; our lips are our own: who is lord over us?"* The wicked are saying, "Whatever we say goes. We are the final authority. We recognize no other authority but our own."

You can say what you want to and end it in a good old "God bless you," but when your heart and your deeds reflect other things, that good old "God bless you" does not work. The Lord contrasts their words with His Word. The Bible says in verses five through seven,

> *For the oppression of the poor, for the sighing of the needy, now will I arise, saith the LORD; I will set him in safety from him that puffeth at him. The words of the LORD are pure words: as silver tried in a furnace of earth, purified seven times. Thou shalt keep them, O LORD, thou shalt preserve them from this generation for ever.*

Our hope is in our God. Our hope is in God's Word. If I did not have God's Word, I would be an even weaker man surrounded by wicked people. It is the strength and sustenance that we get from God's Word that enables us to carry on. We cry out, *"Help, Lord."* Our help is in God and in His Word.

OUR HELP IS IN GOD'S PEOPLE

Notice the occasion of this psalm. Psalm 12:1 says, *"Help, Lord; for the godly man ceaseth; for the faithful fail from among the children of men."* In other words, he is saying, "Lord, what we need is godly men. We need faithful men." This is the need of every hour. Think with me about where the heart of our trouble lies and how we got into this condition.

> *The real heart of the problem in our nation is not the vile, wicked people we hear; it is the silence of God's people.*

On the one hand we see all these things going wrong, and we declare, "This is the problem." I don't think so. The heart of this issue is that we are missing those faithful men who will rise up against what is wrong. The great challenge of this hour is not to point out the wickedness. The great challenge of this hour is to raise up an army that will do right.

How do we apply this to our lives? Are we known as people who stand for righteousness? Everybody who knows the pastor and his ministry ought to know where he stands on every issue. The people should never have to ask, "I wonder what the preacher thinks about this." They ought to know. They ought to know because the preacher has made it plain where he stands. He must do it with compassion, but he must stand.

If it is right for the preacher to do this, it is right for all of God's children to do it. We need to stand in our homes, in our churches, and on our jobs. We need to be faithful to God in every sphere of our lives. We need to be so far removed from wickedness that we never bring reproach to the name of our Lord Jesus Christ by how we live or by what we say.

In II Timothy 2:1-4, Paul writes to his son in the ministry,

> *Thou therefore, my son, be strong in the grace that is in Christ Jesus. And the things that thou hast heard of me among many witnesses, the same commit thou to faithful men, who shall be able to teach others also. Thou therefore endure hardness, as a good soldier of Jesus Christ. No man that warreth entangleth himself with the affairs of this life; that he may please him who hath chosen him to be a soldier.*

Paul said, "Everything that I have taught you, that I have lived for, that I have passed on to you, I want you to teach to faithful men." This is our only hope. In God, in God's Word, and in God's people who will stand, we find our help. The psalmist said, *"Help, Lord."* This wicked, vile age should bring us to our knees, crying out, *"Help, Lord."* This simple prayer composed of two words must continually be in our hearts and on our lips.

Psalm 13

How long wilt thou forget me, O Lord? for ever? how long wilt thou hide thy face from me?

How long shall I take counsel in my soul, having sorrow in my heart daily? how long shall mine enemy be exalted over me?

Consider and hear me, O Lord my God: lighten mine eyes, lest I sleep the sleep of death;

Lest mine enemy say, I have prevailed against him; and those that trouble me rejoice when I am moved.

But I have trusted in thy mercy; my heart shall rejoice in thy salvation.

I will sing unto the Lord, because he hath dealt bountifully with me.

CHAPTER THIRTEEN

HAS GOD FORGOTTEN YOU?

 hen was the last time you complained about what God allowed to come into your life? One day my wife and I came driving up to our house, and we saw a strange looking dog at our door. He was a huge dog, a boxer, an old one, and a very ugly one. Of course I like dogs, I sincerely do. As a matter of fact, my wife has a special affection for pets. But we did not know this dog, and we did not know where he came from. He could only see out of one eye, and I am sure he had been mistreated. I said to my wife, "Honey, look what the Lord has sent us." I did not get a really good response out of her. This dog immediately made himself at home at the front door. He found a place to rest and acted as if he had been there for years.

The dog we had previously owned never even laid down on that step. He thought his God-given responsibility was to terrorize the community. He stole things from everyone's yard, and of course they came to "the preacher's" house to find where their things had gone. He felt it was his responsibility to pick up every child's toy in every neighbor's yard and bring it home to us. The parents of those children felt it was their responsibility to come to our house and talk to "the preacher" about where their children's toys had gone. It did not work well. That dog had to go–it was sad.

> *The real victory in life is not found in the absence of trouble, but rather in the presence of God.*

But this dog was different. He made himself at home. I said to my wife, "Honey, I know you want to take care of him. I am sure he belongs to someone. He looks like someone has given him a little attention, but if you feed him and give him water, he will stay. I don't think he is really hungry, so let's not feed him or give him water and hope that he will go away. If we do, I know he is going to stay." She said, "I don't think I can live if I don't give him some water and something to eat." I said, "Please try not to do that." She fed him!

Of course, that night we went to bed; we were not in bed long before we heard this knocking at the door. It was not a person; it was a paw. He was knocking at the door with his paw. My wife insisted that he was lonely and needed special attention. The next day, he was there to stay. I said, "Look what you've done."

We left during the day and when we came home in the evening, he was gone. She said, "Praise the Lord. He knew I didn't need another dog. Lord, I want to thank you for finding that dog a good home." We no sooner got out of the car and closed the door until he came lumbering out of the woods. He was not gone; he was just up there in the shade waiting for us to return. I said, "Do you think the Lord could have sent this dog?" We came to the conclusion that we did not know whether the Lord or the Devil sent him, but he was there to stay.

THE PLEA OF THE PSALMIST

In your life, there are times when something comes your way and you do not know whether the Lord or the Devil sent it, but it is there. If the Devil sent it, God allowed it for a purpose. As the seasons of life come and go, seek the Lord for His purpose in that season.

The psalmist David said in Psalm 13:1-2, *"How long wilt thou forget me, O LORD? for ever? how long wilt thou hide thy face from me? How long shall I take counsel in my soul, having sorrow in my heart daily? how long shall mine enemy be exalted over me?"*

Again and again we read, *"how long."* He cries out, "How long, Lord." Four times in these two verses he asks, *"how long,"* and once when he finishes saying *"how long,"* he cries out, *"For ever?"*

We really do not know what specific incident occasioned this particular psalm. It is a psalm of David, and we do know that for eight or nine years David was fleeing from the wrath of King Saul. Can you imagine holding up in caves or hiding out in a forest, not for days, weeks or months, but for years? For years, David was unable to travel freely. It began with days, and the days turned to weeks, and the weeks to months, and the months into years. No wonder he said, "How long? Is this the way it is going to be forever?"

The trial is secondary. It is used by God to bring about spiritual strength. These dark hours are required to bring us to a place of dependence upon God.

Do your troubles come to stay? We begin to grumble and our grumbling turns into murmuring against God. David cried out, *"How long wilt thou forget me, O LORD? for ever? how long wilt thou hide thy face from me?"*

If you think you can live without trouble, you are wrong. Anyone who has lived a while can testify to the fact that the Bible is true: *"Man that is born of a woman is of few days, and full of trouble"* (Job 14:1). I hear people in their seventies and eighties say, "Pastor, I didn't think I would have something like this to deal with at my age." Trouble is with us for as long as we are on this earth. The real victory in life is not found in the absence of trouble, but rather in the presence of God.

> *We must get to the place where we take our burdens to the Lord and allow them to become prayers.*

David said, *"How long wilt thou hide thy face from me? How long shall I take counsel in my soul, having sorrow in my heart daily?"* For David, everyday was another day of the same heartache. *"How long shall mine enemy be exalted over me?"*

The Bible says in Isaiah 49:15, *"Can a woman forget her sucking child, that she should not have compassion on the son of her womb?"* Think before you answer! Can a mother forget a child who is still nursing? Can a woman forget such a child, her own child that cannot live without the nourishment from her body? We would answer quickly, "No." But we have lived to see that people not only forget their children, some have even put them to death, exhibiting the most horrible demonstration of unnatural affection.

There is no love on earth like a mother's love, but can a mother forget her child? God answers His own question declaring *"Yea, they may forget, yet will I not forget thee."*

Even though a mother could possibly forget her own child, our God will never forget His children. He says in verse sixteen, *"Behold, I have graven thee upon the palms of my hands; thy walls are continually before me."* We are actually written in the palms of

His hands. God has not forgotten you! Let this verse make a deep impression on your heart.

David said, *"How long wilt thou forget me, O LORD?"* There are times when the Lord allows us to go through trials that challenge and compel us to search for Him. But the Lord has not forgotten us.

THE PRAYER OF THE PSALMIST

In Psalm 13:3, the psalmist cries from his heart, *"Consider and hear me, O LORD my God: lighten mine eyes, lest I sleep the sleep of death."* Note the little word *"lest."* He says, "Lord, I am going to die under this burden if You don't help me."

Have you ever felt you were under so heavy a load that you thought if it was not lifted, it could kill you? The trial is secondary. It is used by God to bring about spiritual strength. These dark hours are required to bring us to a place of dependence upon God. We find comfort and strength that gives us boldness in witnessing to others. The Bible says in II Corinthians 1:3-4,

> *Blessed be God, even the Father of our Lord Jesus Christ, the Father of mercies, and the God of all comfort; who comforteth us in all our tribulation, that we may be able to comfort them which are in any trouble, by the comfort wherewith we ourselves are comforted of God.*

God fully knows what He is doing. The amazing thing in Psalm thirteen is that the plea of the psalmist becomes a prayer. We must get to the place where we take our burdens to the Lord and allow them to become prayers. When they become prayers, God comes to our aid. He is waiting for this pressing issue, this trouble, to become a prayer. He is waiting for us to cry out to Him, seeking Him for help.

It is our nature to want people to know what we are going through and to seek their pity. We are pleased when people know that we are having a hard time. God has not forsaken us. He is here. He will be with us in our trials. Give Him glory. Seek Him and cry out to Him.

Never accept your problems as the end of it all. They are tools in the hand of God to bring us closer to Him. You are not about to fall through the cracks. Look to God by faith.

THE PRAISE OF THE PSALMIST

Psalm 13:5-6 says, *"But I have trusted in thy mercy; my heart shall rejoice in thy salvation. I will sing unto the LORD, because he hath dealt bountifully with me."* We think that we are here, and God is a million miles away. Remember, *"Man that is born of a woman is of few days, and full of trouble."* I do not like to say this, but I am going to have trouble from time to time for the rest of my life and so are you. But God has not given us the spirit of fear. The Bible says in II Timothy 1:7, *"For God hath not given us the spirit of fear; but of power, and of love, and of a sound mind."*

When David begins praising the Lord in this psalm, notice carefully what he emphasizes. *"But I have trusted in thy mercy; my heart shall rejoice in thy salvation. I will sing unto the LORD, because he hath dealt bountifully with me."* Look at who is coupled together, the man and his Lord. *"I have trusted in thy mercy..."* In my Bible, I have circled the pronoun *"I"* and the words *"thy mercy,"* and I have connected *"I"* and *"thy."*

In my Bible, I have circled the word *"my"* in the expression, *"my heart shall rejoice in thy salvation."* And I also circled the word *"thy"* where David says, *"But I have trusted in thy mercy."* At the end of the psalm, David says, *"I will sing unto the LORD, because he hath dealt bountifully with me."* It is no longer, "God has forgotten me." David realizes that God is near.

David's geographical location did not need to change to achieve this victory. He had to put his faith in the Lord. Notice the phrase in verse five, *"But I have trusted in thy mercy."*

What a beautiful verse in I John 5:4. The Bible says, *"For whatsoever is born of God overcometh the world: and this is the victory that overcometh the world, even our faith."* The object of our faith is the Lord Jesus Christ.

How can a child of God sing the Lord's song in the Devil's land? By faith. This is the only way. The Bible says, *"But I have trusted in thy mercy; my heart shall rejoice in thy salvation."* David knew that salvation is wonderful in the present hour. It is not simply a past experience. *"I have trusted...my heart shall..."*

> *Never accept your problems as the end of it all. They are tools in the hand of God to bring us closer to Him.*

The Lord allowed circumstances in David's life to remind him of what he truly possessed in the Lord. *"I will sing unto the Lord, because he hath dealt bountifully with me."* It is one thing to have God deal with you; it is another thing to have God deal bountifully with you.

I need to move from *"How long?"* to *"He hath dealt bountifully with me."* Everyone needs to go from saying, *"How long?"* to saying, *"He hath dealt bountifully with me."*

171